PARTY BASICS FOR
new nesters

More Than
100 Fresh Ideas
for Holidays
and Every Day

MARIA McBRIDE

Photographs by **Alison Rosa**

Collins
An Imprint of HarperCollinsPublishers

To Candy, Russ, Marge, and
Dan, two remarkable couples
and natural nesters

PARTY BASICS FOR NEW NESTERS.
Copyright © 2008 by Maria McBride.
Photographs © 2008 by Alison Rosa.

HarperCollins books may be purchased
for educational, business, or sales
promotional use. For information please
write: Special Markets Department,
HarperCollins Publishers, 10 East 53rd
Street, New York, NY 10022.

FIRST EDITION

Designed by Susi Oberhelman

Library of Congress Cataloging-in-
Publication Data has been applied for.

ISBN 978-0-06-114261-1

08 09 10 11 12 ❖ / TOP 10 9 8 7 6 5 4 3 2 1

contents

INTRODUCTION 8

PARTY BASICS 15

new year's eve

47

lunar new year

65

valentine's day

83

spring fling

95

earth day

109

cinco de mayo

125

flag day

141

labor day

159

halloween

177

thanksgiving

193

winter solstice

211

PARTY REGISTRY   229

RESOURCES   230

CREDITS   238

ACKNOWLEDGMENTS   240

introduction

I've always been a homebody. As the eldest child of a large family, I grew up in a chaotic whirl of activity. Every day had long to-do lists, dozens of schedules to keep on track, yet amazingly almost every night was celebrated around the dinner table. Lucky me—my parents provided us with a cozy home, lots of love, and a blueprint for life: Hug often and embrace each day as if it might be a party. The right partner makes this easier to do. I realized early that celebrations at home need little more than a merry spirit to be a success.

When I married Brett, my father-in-law was not pleased. Brett and I were unemployed college students and madly in love. He warned us, "You'll just be living on LUUVVV!" Instead of mustering a sense of doom, we were delighted with the romantic notion and took pride in feathering our own nest.

Our first dinner party was for my new in-laws. I wanted to prove it was possible to make ends meet—even entertain—when living on love. In a quest to look worldly, I stir-fried shredded pork and wrapped seasoned cabbage into spring rolls, but my hours of effort fell flat. I did impress Brett's parents with my resourcefulness, but his midwestern dad was reluctant to taste anything more exotic than white rice. That day I learned an important lesson about the seductive nature of comfort foods and that I could have simply melted his dad's heart with mashed potatoes.

As newlyweds, it seemed like we were playing house, but I now realize we were practicing living together. Everyday dinners and celebrations helped us define our partnership. Preparing simple meals together and dining by candlelight became our first romantic tradition, but before long we were brazen enough to follow my mom's recipe, stuffing (and deboning!) two turkeys for our first Thanksgiving together—a neighbor's oven made it possible. On the hottest day of the summer, friends would fill the apartment for our Hawaiian party. When we found a home with a deck, dinner under the stars became our specialty and Brett earned his reputation as the grill master.

I believe in daily rituals. Studies show that sharing a meal together is a significant bonding experience. Making memories of comfortable, happy moments is an important emotional building block. Learning how to create celebrations together is a skill that will strengthen your relationship. Working together and enjoying the results is a healthy accomplishment.

Although there are all sorts of nesters (as my mom would croon, *"people who need people . . ."*), I've found that those who have already planned a wedding together are appropriately fearless when it comes to hosting a party. Why not? The experience of organizing hundreds of details makes the prospect of a dinner buffet for six friends seem a snap. Plus, it's a treat to break in all the nifty new housewarming and wedding gifts.

There is an art to party planning—all anyone needs is practice. You'll find the goal of providing a comfortable ambience can be as easy as lighting 30 votives. Remember, even when the night is dressy, the moment should still feel relaxed and natural. A bit of imagination and simple elements are all you really need to set your table any day with style.

Successful celebrations rely on teamwork, a realistic plan, and basic tools. Stock up on elements you'll reuse often, like basic white dinner plates, platters, and candles. A party pantry makes a smart foundation; the following tips will help you focus on the details.

Party Plans

DOORWAY DETAILS are the first element that welcomes guests. You'll want to fit the décor with the season, so consider galvanized tubs brimming with flowering herbs, a holiday wreath of ribbons, or a pile of gilded pumpkins.

MONOCHROMATIC COLOR SCHEMES are a logical organizing concept. Design table accents and even make food selections based on a primary palette.

SEASONAL BOTANICALS make easy decorative building blocks—farm-fresh eggs in the spring, beach treasures for summer, leafy clippings come fall, baskets of pinecones when winter arrives.

FOUND OBJECTS discovered at flea markets and garage sales make sensational decorative accents. I've picked up copper buckets, plaster urns, period tableware, vintage linens, retro coolers, and garden seating.

ENHANCE LIGHTING. Turn off fluorescent lights for celebrations (it's just too clinical). Install ceiling light dimmers and opt for candles and more candles.

CHEAP THRILLS are everywhere. Keep shopping sales on your radar and stash fun finds in your pantry, like cotton dishtowels to use as napkins, colorful straws, or bags of tea lights, all easily found at dollar stores and home furnishing and accessory emporiums.

PROFESSIONAL SUPPLIERS are excellent sources of well-priced, useful tools, tableware, and decorative accents.

MAKE LISTS. Logistics are more manageable with a to-do list. You should have three main lists: a shopping list with recipes, a phone or e-mail list with guests contacts, and a simple countdown list for the three days before each party.

MANAGEABLE CROWDS make the most sense. Keep guest lists reasonable; don't overwhelm your space, your sanity, or your budget.

DRESS CODE CLUES should be given to your guests with the invitation. As hosts, you'll set the tone. Suggest "easy" or "dressy" and be sure to give yourselves plenty of time for your own pampering before guests arrive; it's the best way to feel calm and collected.

GET HELP FOR LARGE PARTIES: College kids and students from bartending schools can lend an affordable hand. Just tell them how to dress—khakis or black trousers always look right.

EXTRA NEEDS like chairs and tables are easily rented from party suppliers. If you have storage space, shop online, at tag sales, and at flea markets for additional seating.

DON'T RUSH—allow two to three hours for most cocktail parties, three to four hours for dinners. Allow up to an hour for drinks and hors d'oeuvres before serving the meal.

SPACE MANAGEMENT is a science but you can look like a whiz if you eliminate bottlenecks. Keep bars away from doorways. Turn a dining table into a buffet so guests can approach from two sides. Remove dining chairs and scatter them in other rooms to create seating nooks.

A BATHROOM CHECK before guests arrive is important. Keep one of the most crucial rooms in the house ready with extra toiletries. A clean bar of soap, fresh towels, extra toilet tissue, and a scented candle are thoughtful and, for insurance, be sure plumbing aids are under the sink.

STOCK ICE. You'll want plenty, so allow two pounds per guest—three for a cocktail-heavy party. Local ice houses deliver for large parties; ask about crushed ice for specialty drinks.

SIGNATURE COCKTAILS are the easiest way to serve a crowd, strike a festive mood, and save money. There's no need to offer a full bar; invite guests for "margaritas and nachos" or simply serve wine or beer. Make clever selections—hometown microbrews for a football match or a mix of white wines for a midsummer night.

EAT SEASONALLY for the most delicious menus. Shop farmers markets for healthy, sustainably produced foods—and flowers, too.

SIMPLE COURSES are best when serving a sit-down meal. A creamy soup that can be prepared ahead and served at the last minute will look smart and keep you sane.

FAST FOODS MAKE SENSE. Can't cook? No time? Who cares! Prepared foods are a delicious timesaving option, easy to order and pick up—just use your own platters to display.

BITE-SIZED HORS D'OEUVRES are crowd pleasers, so be sure to stock plenty. For cocktail parties with 8 to 10 guests, serve 3 options; estimate that each person will eat 2 or 3 of each. For 14 to 16 guests, serve 4 or 5 hors d'oeuvres; for 20 to 30 guests, serving 7 or 8 options is most festive, but calculate that each guest will only have 1 or 2 servings of each taste.

MOOD MUSIC soothes the soul and enlivens any party. Strive for a moderate background level. Be mindful of your neighbors and guests; music shouldn't be so loud that it's difficult to

have a conversation. Mix an upbeat rhythm for cocktails, but mellow is best for meals. For holidays, seek out soundtracks, folk songs, world music, or even kitschy tracks. A clever variety makes for a more memorable celebration.

WELCOME GUESTS with a hearty hello and make introductions. Mingle but plan to scoot in and out of the kitchen all night. As hosts you'll take turns greeting guests and catering to their needs.

CLEAN UP AS YOU GO. Professionals know that it's the best way to keep from being overwhelmed in the kitchen. Better yet, pretreat messes. Use sections of wax paper as work mats—just toss when done. A spritz of nonstick spray on cooking surfaces, spoons, graters, and mixing bowls when you're using gooey ingredients will be a big help. Keep towels handy. For stubborn kitchen messes, mix three parts of baking soda with one part water. Apply, let soak, and wipe up.

PAMPER PETS. If your home has the sounds of the pitter-patter of little feet, take the time to focus on their needs before guests arrive, and keep treats and toys handy to calm nerves. Excitable critters may even need some private space.

STEAL A KISS for good luck and love. After all, that's why you're hosting a party—to celebrate your togetherness.

party basics

Despite all the details to organize, parties really are a snap
to pull off when you focus on the basics. If you master a few simple
skills, stock your pantry with the right utensils, learn where to
find the right staples, make lists, and keep them doable, you'll find
it easy to be a host. Entertaining well is a learnable skill. The more
you do it, the easier it becomes. You'll find celebrations for two or
parties for many more require the same elements. Nesters should
rejoice—you have a partner with whom you can split the tasks
and master the techniques. So you have no excuse: Have a party!

INVITATIONS

In many ways, the invitation is the most complicated element of hosting a party; simply choosing a date that works is tricky. Luckily, creating a clever request is a snap. Although it's completely appropriate to use e-mail to invite guests, everyone enjoys receiving an invitation in the mail. For sanity's sake, keep it simple. The right materials will make it easy to look smart.

Picking a date that fits your schedules is the first task. As anyone who's planned a wedding knows, you need to give guests plenty of notice. E-mail save-the-dates when you're planning a large gathering. Write a simply worded note with the time and occasion about 6 weeks before the date, select a font and color to suit the season, and send. Follow up with complete details by mail 3 weeks before the celebration. For smaller gatherings, you can allow a shorter time frame. Major reunions likely need 6 months—even a year during the busiest seasons.

PAPER Quality stock simply feels good in your hand. Stationery emporiums offer a wonderland of options. I prefer note cards that are 4 inches by 6 inches or smaller. They are typically sold with complementary envelopes. Colors that signify the season are the best selections. For something more whimsical, kraft paper, cardboard stock, even index cards work well. Use photographs or prints to personalize.

INKS To make text legible there should be a contrast between the ink color and the paper. Black, brown, and navy inks look best on cream, white, and pale tones. White ink is dramatic on black and brown papers. Calligraphy markers—with a thin and a thick felt nib at each end— come in more colors than Crayola crayons, making it easy to customize the design of your invitation.

RUBBER STAMPS Quickly inked images and letters make fast work of production. Ink pads come in a wide range of colors. I like to mix rubber stamps and markers for a collage-like composition. Order custom self-inking stamps with your initial or message for professional flourish.

SEALS Use a metal stamp to emboss a puddle of wax for sealing envelopes, or try adhesive dots or vinyl decals, which can also be used to punctuate your composition. Detail paper dots with a rubber stamp for a clever monogram.

EMBOSSER This tool has a customizable plate that stamps paper with raised impressions— great for monograms.

FLOWERS

Unquestionably, fresh blooms add a festive touch to our daily life and are required table dressing for any special event. Happily, every season introduces a vivacious crop to tempt us to turn our living rooms into lush gardens. I shop at farmers markets, my neighborhood flower shop, nurseries, even the corner food market, since all of them regularly stock cut flowers. If the price is right I'll load up on extra bunches and crowd several vases for an indulgent display.

Before you buy any flowers, a **brief inspection** will ensure that you select the best bunch. Look for viable green foliage that doesn't look wilted. Stems should be firm; if they're limp, their vascular tissue has already started to deteriorate and the flowers will be short-lived.

Once you get home, a little preparation will maximize the life of your arrangement. First, be sure your vase is clean. A **soapy rinse** with warm water will remove any trace of bacterial contaminants from the container.

Fill the vessel halfway with clear, cool water. Remove excess and damaged foliage from each stem. I leave only the best-looking leaves that emerge closest to the neck of the flower and pluck all the remaining leaves with a firm pinch between my fingertips. Be sure to **remove all** leaves that will rest below the water line. By trimming the excess foliage you optimize the life of the plant stem. The stem is a series of thin, strawlike tubes that draw water to the plant cells; eliminating unnecessary greenery will ensure water goes directly to the flower head.

Use a clean, sharp pair of clippers or a floral knife to make a fresh cut to the flower stem. (Dull blades crush stems and vascular vessels.) **Clip off** at least 2 inches from the base to remove any damaged or dried stem, more to accommodate short vases. Cut at a 45-degree angle to optimize the absorption surface of the stem; a slant cut maximizes the water intake area. If the plant has a woody stem—a lilac, for instance—make an additional inch-long cut up the center of the stem.

Replenish water as needed—the stems are alive only as long as they are drinking—and replace the water if it becomes cloudy. Check the stems: If the ends seem mushy or hardened, cut off the deteriorated section and return to the vase with fresh water. **Pluck out** any stems that prematurely fade, and keep the blooms away from intense sources of heat, like radiators or windows with southern exposures. With a little TLC, fresh flowers will last up to a week.

floral tools

1. OASIS Lightweight water-absorbing foam, manufactured especially for floral design, is widely available in floral and craft supply shops (as are all of the items on this page). The foam comes in a variety of sizes meant to fit easily into vases or any container. To use, presoak the foam in a pot filled with clean water. Once saturated, the foam can be placed into your container. Insert the cut stems of your flowers directly into the foam for a source of water and stability.

2. SCISSORS Short blades and wide, looped handles are the design hallmark of Japanese-style shears originally crafted for bonsai trimming. The open handles are easy to grip, and the short blades are ideal for cutting ribbons or trimming leaves and flowers.

3. TAPE Self-adhesive floral tape will stick only to itself, so it's perfect for bundling stems together into bouquets. Use with floral wire to create pliable stems when making wreaths. It's slightly stretchy, so pull the tape taut for a smooth finish.

4. CLIPPER An arched blade cradles the flower stem so that it's a cinch to cut. Opt for a pair with comfort-grip handles and a spring coil to ease the repetitive task of clipping.

5. WIRE Spools of floral wire are handy when decorating wreaths. Hold the spool in one hand and twist an inch or so around the neck of an object to be used, then wind the spool around the wreath frame to attach the object. Use clippers to cut wire.

6. KNIFE You'll find this folding knife in every florist's pocket. Hold it securely in your dominant hand to guide the cut away from your body. When cleaning flowers that are fresh from the market or garden, use the knife to remove any damaged leaves and all foliage that rests below the water line. Cut where the leaf meets the stem.

7. FROG This metal weight with sharp spikes, known by an unlikely name—perhaps because it squats in a vase underwater just as its amphibian namesake does—is meant to anchor flower stems. Skewer the stem to the frog exactly where you want it to stand. Scour flea markets for vintage versions of looped wire or domes pockmarked with thimble-sized holes meant for flower stems.

easy centerpiece

When I want a fast infusion of flowers in my life I usually just toss a bunch of one type of flower into my favorite container, but sometimes—for more formal celebrations or to send as a special treat to my family or friends—I want to put together a look that is a mix of the season's best. If you combine compatible stems in a simple vase, it's easy to create a floral arrangement that looks like it's been freshly delivered from a florist.

I've learned from florist friends that it's best to build your arrangement starting with the heaviest stems. I like to use woody stems like lilac, because their typically fluffy heads make a lush base. Add a few sturdy-stemmed flowers, like the rose, for structure. Finish with a similar amount of soft-stemmed blooms, like tulips, for punctuation.

1. Fill an 8-inch-square vase to the midpoint with clear water. Clean and prep stems of 9 lilacs, 6 stems roses, 6 stems tulips.

2. One by one, place all the stems of the lilac in the vase, using a crisscross pattern to create a balanced framework.

3. Insert the roses randomly throughout the lilac nest, clustering a couple of the roses in the same area for a more natural appearance.

4. Add tulips; scatter and place so the flower heads have room to open up without overlapping the roses. Spin the vase and tweak the placement of the flowers until the look is appealing from all sides.

CANDLES

Any time you light a candle, it's an instant party. I can't imagine entertaining at night without candlelight. Routine dinners become a romantic rendezvous, a cocktail party tilts swank, backyard barbecues become feasts to remember, all because of these wicked wicks. I always buy candles in bulk—bags of tea lights or tapers by the box—so that I can turn any evening into a celebration.

There are numerous candle options on the market today. Most commercially available candles are made with paraffin (a petroleum by-product), beeswax, or a blend of the two. If you prefer a more ecologically sensitive option, use soy candles. Many candles are scented; these are lovely in the entry hall, bathroom, or bedroom, but I prefer unscented candles when serving food to avoid overpowering the senses. For parties I **scatter** candles throughout the house so the mood isn't broken when guests step into other rooms. Don't forget the bathroom: Fill your tub with a few inches of water and float candles for a delightful ambience. Candles come in every color, which I love, but I stock basic white and off-white because they are ubiquitous, affordable, and always appropriate.

If you are using new tapers or pillars, before your party, trim the wick to ¼ inch, then briefly light until a tiny puddle of wax appears, then extinguish. **Conditioning** the candle this way will make it easier to relight quickly moments before your guests arrive. I keep a butane torch handy for easy igniting, but in a pinch, a strand of uncooked spaghetti can stand in for a long match. If your candle burns unevenly it's because of a draft; rotate the candle so it burns uniformly or move it to another location.

If you need to **adjust** the fit of tapers to your candlestick, try one of these tricks: If tapers wiggle a tiny bit, drip a puddle of wax into the socket to secure it in place. Keep a tiny tin of soft candle wax handy, available where candles are sold. Roll a pea-sized bead between the candle and socket to wedge the candle in place or a use a swatch of aluminum foil to wrap the bottom of the candle for a better fit. If the candle is too large, use a fruit peeler to shave a thick strip from the base to correct the fit.

Blow out candles by holding your finger to your lips as though you are saying "shhhh"; this prevents splattering wax with the force of your breath. Gently lift dried wax off table surfaces with the edge of an old credit card. Add a teaspoon of water to the bottom of votive cups before placing the candle inside to ease removal of the spent candle or, once it's used, fill the votive holders with water to loosen the wax for a quick cleanup.

SHAPELY SELECTIONS (*left to right*): **1.** large floater; **2.** battery-powered LED that flickers when on—perfect for drafty locations; **3.** thin birthday taper; **4.** traditional taper; **5.** beeswax taper; **6.** square pillar; **7.** white matchboxes under glass votives poured with wax; **8.** round pillar; **9.** tea lights in clear plastic sleeves that disappear in any votive holder; **10.** 15-hour votive; **11.** small floater; and **12.** 8-hour votive.

votives

Two inches tall but mighty versatile, these plain glass cylinders can be used just out of the box, but in minutes you can decorate them to suit your mood. They're affordable and available by the case from a kitchen or florist supplier—I suggest you buy at least 24 votives, but more is better. Scatter them about your home, clustered in odd-numbered groups on any flat surface.

1. STICKER Customize a round dot (from office suppliers and stationery stores) with a monogram. Using a rubber stamp, I inked an olive circle with my initial before applying it to the glass.

2. RIBBON Around the center of the glass, coil 9 inches of thin satin ribbon in a color that suits your celebration. Tie it off with a simple knot.

3. GOOGLY EYES Plastic domes that hold little black discs are sold in craft shops in several sizes. For Halloween, I attached a dozen of the smallest eyes with glue for a whimsical spin on spooky.

4. ADHESIVE Peel-and-stick letters are available in a variety of colorful fonts at craft centers. Use initials for a monogram or spell out words to personalize the glass with phrases.

5. VINYL Order miniature peel-and-stick letters or patterns from the same sign specialists who create dance floor decorations.

6. COPPER LEAF Rub on tissue-thin sheets of metal to surfaces that are tacky with adhesive spray; the reflective results make this idea a holiday favorite. Packages of metal leaf are available in gold, silver, or copper at craft suppliers.

7. MONOGRAM Block letters, available at fabric and notions shops, can adhere to glass with craft glue. This varsity look is terrific for tailgate parties and reunions.

8. WALLPAPER Wrap 6 inches of patterned wallpaper trim (available at home improvement centers) and secure with a 2-inch strip of double-stick tape. Use a hole-punch to cut peepholes in the paper.

9. VINE Twist 20 inches of wired faux grapevine (available at craft centers) around the glass for harvest season holidays or wine tastings.

BARWARE

A few key elements will meet all your bartending needs. Clear glassware gets my vote as the most versatile investment—it mixes with any décor, all tableware, any mood, and will look smart for a generation of celebrations.

1. SHAKER Fill this cylinder with ice and mixers, and top with perforated lid and cap. Shake to chill a cocktail thoroughly. The design of the lid strains the ice to pour a neat drink.

2. ICE BUCKET It's impossible to have a swell cocktail without ice. An ice bucket is an elegant and practical addition to any party and, depending on your needs, it can also be used as a vase or wine cooler. Serve cubes with tongs or a scoop for quick, clean service. To be sure you have plenty of ice for chilling and mixing, calculate two pounds of ice per person for a party. Stock backup ice in a picnic cooler, in a clean trash can lined with a plastic bag, or in a bathtub.

3. CARAFE Decant wines and serve mixed drinks, water, or even candies with a swish. Carafes allow a wine to open, or breathe, as it is poured from the bottle. Fans of robust, unfiltered wines are smart to open bottles 30 minutes before drinking, but any bottle of wine benefits from being decanted, allowing complex and subtle flavors in the wine to breathe and become more expressive.

bar tools

I admire the ingenious nature of simple tools designed to make tasks a breeze. My favorites are efficient, and feel comfortable in the hand.

1. MUDDLER This wood baton has a griddled base, perfect for pulverizing mint leaves for mojitos and mint juleps, lime wedges for *caipirinhas*, and berries for daiquiris. Add ingredients to a mixing glass and mash with the muddler; you can mix with sugar to make a sweet paste.

2. STRAINER Slotted with rabbit ears, this metal restrainer is designed to hold ice cubes in a mixing glass while straining the cocktail mix into a drinking glass.

3. MIXING SPOON The tool to use when a recipe calls for stirring. The long spiral stem creates an ideal wave to mix drinks. When layering drinks, pour successive liqueurs over the back of the spoon, held upside down, against the inside of the glass.

4. MIXING GLASS Stir or shake drinks with a large mixing glass; 24 ounces is best. To turn it into a shaker, use a smaller glass as a topper—its rim should fit inside the large glass. Hold the two glasses together to seal the vessel, and shake vigorously.

5. CORKSCREW Remove corks easily with these mechanical rabbit ears. Twist the tip of the drill into the cork, then hold the chamber around the bit tight to the bottle and use your other hand to turn the gear until the ears are erect. Pull back the ears to remove the cork.

6. SHOT GLASS All drink recipes call for an ounce or fractions of an ounce of ingredients. A glass with identifying measurements makes it easy to measure.

7. STOPPERS Rubberized plugs make a tight seal for wine bottles; the handle is easy to use. Champagne caps clip on to the neck of the bottle to preserve the bubbles and keep the stopper in place.

8. BOTTLE OPENER Removing metal caps and puncturing tin lids are easier with the leverage of a sturdy handle. Contents pour smoothly if lids are cut with two opposite openings (make one a smaller wedge to allow air to flow).

9. CAPTAIN'S KNIFE This is widely used by waiters and bartenders who appreciate a tool that folds easily and slips safely into a pocket. It's also handy for picnics and travel. A retractable knife point makes it easy to remove foil caps from wine bottles. Extend the spiral point at a 90-degree angle from the handle to twist into the center of the cork. Brace the hinge against the lip of the bottle to extract the cork.

10. REAMER Juice citrus fruits of all sizes with this old-fashioned tool. After slicing the fruit in half, push the tool into the pulp to break the membranes and releases the juices.

11. ZESTER Harvest a long strip of citrus skin (wash the fruit first) with this tool. The stainless blade cuts a shallow trench through the skin to create the strand. Some zesters also have a row of five small stainless steel circles sharpened to cut thinner threads.

12. CUTTING BOARD Dishwasher-safe acrylic chopping boards make easy cleanup.

good garnishes

A tasty cocktail mixes fresh fruits, premium mixers, the right amount of ice, and liquor for a delicious concoction. The perfect cocktail is served in a chilled glass garnished with a flourish—a smart accent that's meant to look as good as it tastes.

SIDECAR A wedge or a slice of citrus notched with a knife to hang on the rim of the glass.

TWIST Citrus skin is rich with essential oils. Peel a ribbon with a zester. Twist then float the coil to flavor the cocktail.

ZEST Create a fine confetti of thin threads shaved from the skin of a citrus fruit or a block of chocolate. Shave the surface with the zester's row of sharp circles.

FLOATING FLOWERS Showy edible blooms include the pansy, rose, carnation, nasturtium, geranium, lavender, and orchid (use them only if they were grown without pesticides). Soak them in a bath of cool water to wash well; dry on a cookie rack.

FANCY ICE CUBES Using ice decoratively puts a crucial ingredient to good use. Freeze berries, mint leaves, or juices to make pretty cubes, or serve drinks with crushed ice for a marbled appearance.

FRUITS AND VEGGIES The produce aisle is stocked with cocktail accessories. The garnish you select should be an essence of the drink or a natural complement. My favorites: olives, canned onions, celery, scallions, Key limes, herbs, and fruits that freeze well to use as ice cubes, like raspberries, grapes, and melon balls.

SWIZZLE STICKS Stirrers add a sexy but practical note to your drink; an occasional stir as you sip keeps the drink uniformly cool and blended. Add a whimsical note with paper goods—make your own or find packaged petite parasols, perfect for tropical cocktails. Use local, national, and nautical flags for drinks served at reunions, or cultural or patriotic holidays.

JEWELED RIM Tinted sugars, coarse salt, edible metal leaf, cinnamon, and ground pepper all make sensational rim decorations. Use a wedge of citrus to coat the rim of the glass with a sticky surface before dipping into a saucer of granulated garnish to decorate the glass with color and flavor. Use corn syrup instead of a slice of citrus when you need a stronger bond for heavier shavings of coconut, chocolate, or ground coffee.

classic cocktails

Shaken, stirred, layered, neat, or on the rocks—select a signature cocktail for your party to coordinate with the holiday, the season, the reason for, or the flavor of your celebration. Save time and mix a pitcher's worth of the evening's brew for many guests. Here are six versatile recipes that are easy to skew to your taste. Be sure to stock chilled glasses in the freezer.

Cosmopolitan

1½ ounces of citrus vodka

½ ounce of Triple Sec

¼ ounce lime juice

½ ounce pomegranate juice

Add all ingredients to a cocktail shaker full of ice. Shake and strain. Garnish with raspberries and pomegranate seeds.

Bloody Mary

1½ ounces of vodka

¼ teaspoon hot prepared horseradish

5 drops Worcestershire sauce

¼ ounce of lime juice

twist of fresh ground pepper

8 ounces tomato juice

salted celery stalk

Fill chilled glass with ice. Add all ingredients except tomato juice and celery. Stir. Add tomato juice. Stir with celery stick.

Daiquiri

1½ ounces of rum

1 ounce simple syrup

1 ounce fresh lime juice

Add all ingredients to a cocktail shaker full of ice. Shake and serve on the rocks or strain to serve neat. Garnish with a slice of lemon and sprig of mint. For fun, use a lemon lollipop as a stirrer.

SIMPLE SYRUP

Combine equal parts sugar and water in a saucepan. Simmer to mix; cool before use.

. . . and more

Martini

2 ounces gin or vodka

¼ ounce dry vermouth

Add all ingredients to a cocktail shaker full of ice; shake and strain or serve over ice and stir. Traditional garnish options are olives for a musky martini or lemon twists for one with a burst of citrus. If served with pickled pearl onions, it's called a Gibson. Or spice it up with a pepperocini.

Sangria

1 bottle of your favorite white wine

juice of 2 limes and 2 lemons

4 ounces simple syrup

16 ounces seltzer or ginger ale, according to taste

1 bunch grapes, washed, separated from vine

lemon zest

Fill pitcher with ice. Add wine, citrus juice, and syrup. Stir well. Add soda, fruit, and lemon zest.

Mojito

1½ ounces of light rum

4 lime wedges

3 teaspoons sugar

4 mint sprigs

splash seltzer

Muddle the limes, sugar, and 3 mint springs in a shaker. Add ice and rum, and shake. Serve over cracked ice, with mint and slices of lime. Splash with seltzer.

wine notes

The more you taste, the more you'll appreciate the complex subtleties of fermented grape juice. Touring wineries together is fabulous way to explore and to refine your palate. Establishing a relationship with a well-stocked wine store in your community is another smart way to start your education. I like to buy wine by the case; the local merchant mixes our favorites and the shop's finds of the month. We keep our receipts and highlight favorites, making it easier for him to match our taste next time. And we always keep bottles of bubbly and white wine in the fridge for spontaneous celebrations.

CHILLING Serving wine too cold will mask the flavors. Most white wines will taste best if refrigerated for 2 hours or submerged for 20 minutes in an ice bath that's equal parts cold water and ice. Beaujolais, light Pinot Noir, and Chianti taste best barely cool; 15 minutes in the fridge will do. Most red wines are best served at room temperature.

COLOR Whether wine becomes white or red depends on the amount of contact the juice has with skins and seeds when they are crushed. Whites are immediately separated from the pulp before fermenting, reds are steeped with the pulp for weeks, and rosés merely hours or days.

CORKS AND CAPS The traditional cork is rapidly being replaced by the screw cap, an efficient closure that opens with an easy twist and eliminates spoilage from a tainted cork.

COST Aficionados may splurge on wines valued at hundreds of dollars, but excellent wines are available for under $20 a bottle and tasty, drinkable, everyday wines can be found for half that. Wine stores and wineries offer case discounts. When looking for real deals, consider warehouse stores, like Costco, which happens to sell the most wine in the country, passing the savings to customers.

GLASSWARE Opt for a clear, wide bowl—16 to 22 ounces is best—that allows plenty of room to swirl the wine and show off its color. Whites stay cooler in smaller bowls. Use skinny flutes for sparkling wines to allow bubbles to rise and dance. Wine-specific glasses are fun for enthusiasts.

LABELS The region, the variety of grape, the winemaker and importer, the year or vintage that the grapes were harvested and bottled, and the alcoholic

REDS   SPARKLING   BIG BOUQUETS   WHITES

content can be found here. Look for regional designations of excellence. For example, superior wines grown in France will be noted as *grand cru* or *premier cru*. Save labels to track your favorites in a wine journal.

TASTE Evaluate color and clarity first with a generous swirl of the glass that also gives the flavor a chance to open up after being in the bottle. The swirl coats the sides of the glass so you can better appreciate aromatic notes. To savor the bouquet, place your nose in the glass and inhale deeply. Finally, take a generous sip and swish the wine in your mouth so it coats the tongue, making it easier for your taste buds to identify and enjoy the flavors of the wine.

STORAGE Store bottles on their side to keep corks moist. Opt for a cool, constant temperature, away from sunlight. Leftover wine keeps well when corked and refrigerated for a few days. Or save it for cooking—just freeze it in ice cube trays for later use.

QUANTITY One bottle of wine easily serves two people for dinner, yielding 5 to 6 glasses. For parties, estimate half a bottle per person. The magnum is a celebration-sized bottle, equivalent to two 750 ml bottles of wine.

VARIETALS This refers to the name of a type of grape. New World wines (bottled anywhere but Europe) are named for their predominant grape: chardonnay,

merlot, cabernet, sauvignon blanc, pinot noir, zinfandel.

REGIONS Wine cultivation has been regulated for centuries in Europe. These Old World wines are identified by their growing region, each distinguished by grapes suited to the climate. Champagne is an area of France where sparkling wine is made, but sparkling wines made outside of this region cannot be labeled Champagne. Other renowned regions: Bordeaux, Burgundy, Chablis, Beaujolais, Chianti, Rioja, Barolo.

WINE STAINS Remove dark wine stains with a mix of equal parts hydrogen peroxide and Dawn liquid soap.

TABLE TIPS

Glasses, plates, and flatware are the basic elements of every table setting. Go basic, go classic, go dressy, go wild—if you have the right elements you can do it all.

Formal tables are set with all the tableware needed for a deluxe meal that includes several courses. When registering for gifts or adding to your collection (I love flea markets, craft fairs, and fashionable-furnishing emporiums to find elements with both personality and practicality), shop for a formal table while opting for versatile elements that can also be used casually.

Traditionalists select tableware in a uniform style and pattern, but I prefer a more spirited blend that makes it easy to change the character of your table to suit your needs and a variety of celebrations.

Whatever your style, start with a large white **dinner plate** (one with texture or simply banded

with gold or platinum is a smart choice), then mix in a bold **accent plate** that can be used for salads, desserts, snacks, or sandwiches. A **soup bowl** with presence can also serve cereal and ice cream.

Flatware is typically sold in 5-piece sets to accommodate a formal table and multiple needs. **Butter knives** are a smart investment. On a formal table you'll serve it on a saucer that doubles as a **bread plate** when positioned to the left of the dinner plate. The same knife is also handy for serving paté, spreads, and jams. The smaller fork is meant to be used with the first course if it's set farthest from the plate. If soup is a first course, set the spoon to the right of the dinner knife. A **dessert spoon** or fork rests at the top of the plate.

Goblets for wine, water, and champagne are all you really need, but feel free to mix the patterns, mix cut crystal with glass, or even mix stem heights to suit your fancy and create a more animated setting. On the formal table, glassware for water is positioned above the dinner knife, followed to the right with wine glasses. Traditionally, red wine is served with the main course and white or champagne with the first selection. Position stemware in a row with the glass for the wine to be enjoyed first set farthest to the right.

Mini-**salt-and-pepper** shakers make a dramatic presence, reminding us that even the littlest details make a big statement.

PANTRY

Stock your shelves with a few basics to be party-ready. Items that you use every day will be the most versatile, and if you select classic styles, you'll get the most value from any dollar you spend. In the long run, you'll easily supplement and update your service ware anytime if the core of your collection is basic white.

A dozen large, white **dinner plates** will give you maximum mileage for all sorts of entertaining. Chefs love them because they frame food beautifully.

White linen **napkins**, 20 inches square, provide generous coverage and launder well. For every day, a durable 2-ply dinner-sized napkin always looks smart. Keep a stack of bright paper cocktail napkins on hand for last-minute parties.

Stock several large **serving bowls** to serve foods family-style or to improvise a centerpiece of floating petals. Indispensable porcelain platters, wood boards, and metal trays will serve meats, breads, cheeses, even drinks.

Six sets of premium **flatware** will get you started. Sterling silver is a swell purchase and, contrary to common belief, is durable enough to use every day. More affordable but equally handsome silverplate and stainless are dishwasher-friendly, as is sterling if handled with care. When I find a sale on flatware that blends in well, I add to my collection.

Traditional **goblets, wineglasses,** and **flutes** are worthy investments; sets of 6 to dress a table will do for most gatherings. I like to stock up on stemless flutes for parties; they're easy to stash in the freezer until ready and the round bottom is tip-proof.

Popular home-furnishing emporiums always stock the latest "thrills," so keep an eye out for sales or supplement your pantry with staples from restaurant suppliers. Embellish your party pantry with **affordable collectibles**, like printed pitchers, that you find at flea markets or online. These add clever flourishes to your table.

seasonings

Spice up take-out food or spend hours braising—the satisfaction of adding flavor to your dining experience is a matter of keeping seasonings handy. Our grandmothers knew this; their favorites lined their stoves. Basic restaurant shakers make it easy to keep your favorite condiments handy, too.

1. METAL SHAKERS
Dust desserts or thicken sauces with a shake; these are just the thing for confectioners' sugar, cornstarch, or flour.

2. SQUEEZE BOTTLE
Drizzle plates with blended oils or fruit purees—both so easy to make yourself—to create a professional finish.

3. GRINDER Crack pepper and coarse salt easily with these classic mills.

4. GLASS BOTTLES
Empty shakers come in many sizes and with a variety of hole options, convenient for cinnamon, chocolate, sesame seeds, red pepper, saffron, and assorted salts. Shop ethnic grocers to find other authentic spices and containers.

食卓塩

TABLE SALT

100g

new year's eve

Some people prefer to jostle with the crowds in Times Square or go to a fancy restaurant on New Year's Eve, but I don't want to be anywhere but home. Of all the celebrations of the year, this is the one that makes me feel most like a grown-up: It's a night meant to start late, to pull out all the stops, to dress up—and it ends with a kiss and maybe more. To fit the sparkly mood, I adorn the house with silver accents and plan a late-night buffet. Guests appreciate plenty of notice for this night, so invite them early in December to drink a toast to auld lang syne.

silver wreath

Greet guests before you even answer the door with a shimmering wreath of ornaments that clearly announces: We're celebrating! I needed about 100 ornaments, so I waited for reduced prices after Christmas. If the price is right, buy extras to fill vases.

MATERIALS

1. Remove the cap and ring of each ornament. Apply a dab of hot glue into the neck of the ornament to attach one wire stem. Let cool and harden.

2. Wrap the neck of the ornament with 2 inches of silver tape to conceal the attachment.

3. Twist 2 ornaments securely together where the wires meet the necks. Continue to twist the wires together to create 1 stem. Set aside until all ornaments have been paired.

4. Twist stem of each ornament bundle around the frame. (Each frame is formed by 4 concentric rings of wire.) Twist each bundle of ornaments around 2 of the rings. Twist tightly into place so that the balls lie snugly against the frame. Continue to attach all the bundles to the frame. Adjust the bundles so that the ornaments fit closely together.

5. Use the last stem of wire to create a hanging loop on the back of the wreath.

100 ornaments—50 clear and 50 silver—or your favorite combination

hot glue gun

3 hot glue sticks

silver tape

101 stems: 8-inch segments of 20-gauge silver wire

1 12-inch wreath frame

crystal vase

'Tis the season to twinkle. When I really want to make the candlelight bounce around the room, I add a layer of bling. Swarovski flat-back silvered crystals are faceted, like rare gems, and easily transform a plain-Jane vase into a glamorous vessel. Clear craft epoxy glues for nonporous materials, like glass, will make the application easy. Once you're done, let the beads and the glue set for 24 hours. Float a candle in blue-tinted water—a couple of drops of food coloring does the trick—or fill with flowers for a dazzling display.

MATERIALS

1 pedestal vase with 5-inch base

clear craft epoxy glue for nonporous material

65 flat-back crystals (allow about 9 8.5mm beads per square inch of surface area)

1. Clean vase.
2. Use a dot of epoxy to attach the crystals to the glass. Start at the center around the stem of the vase to attach the first stone.
3. Place each stone adjacent to another to blanket the base.
4. Once the area is covered with crystals, set aside overnight.

confetti tray

I love to find unusual uses for everyday items. One day, while buying a frame for a photograph, it occurred to me that the frame was the same size as a standard serving tray and the picture area allowed for all sorts of customizing opportunities. The most affordable frames are available in simple styles and basic colors. Slip confetti between two panes of glass to frame a sparkly constellation. Toss extra on the tabletop and—since you'll have to run the vacuum cleaner anyway—have extra bowls ready to toss at midnight. It's a night made for confetti.

MATERIALS

scissors

8-inch x 11-inch sheet silver paper

1¼-inch square or star-shaped paper punch

glass cleaning solution

paper towels

11-inch x 14-inch panes of precut glass

white wood frame with 11-inch x 14-inch opening

1-inch putty knife

8 glazing points

1. Cut sheet of silver paper into 2-inch strips. Use the paper punch to cut out confetti from the paper strips. (Or look for a 2-ounce bag of silver spangles at a party supply store.) Set aside.

2. Spray glass cleaner directly onto a paper towel to clean the glass panes. (To remove any lint that might remain, a ball of crumpled newspaper may be more effective against static than the paper towel.)

3. Turn the frame upside down. Remove any hardware from the back of the frame so the tray will lie flat on a tabletop. Insert 1 pane of glass into the frame. Scatter plenty of confetti across the glass, then insert the second pane of glass.

4. Use a putty knife to insert 2 glazing or framing points into each side of the frame to hold the glass securely in place. Position each point 2 inches from each corner; the flat side of the point should rest directly on the glass with the tip pointed toward the frame. The notch of the points will fit against the blade of the knife—simply push the point into the wood.

MAKES 1 TRAY

midnight buffet

Invite guests to arrive at 9 P.M.—later is best, since the highlight of the evening is midnight. You'll love having more time to set up and dress up, too. Buffets are a convivial presentation, and when guests can serve themselves it's easier to accommodate a crowd. But you need lots of extras: a generous stack of dinner plates, a platter of flatware, and plenty of glassware for serving drinks, champagne, dessert, and coffee. Rental companies provide all these extras, even linens, at a fraction of the cost of purchasing more, and they'll even wash the dishes! Mixing high style—candelabra and tapers—with low elements on your buffet instantly creates a more dramatic presentation. Instead of a basic ice bucket, a stone garden urn can hold several bottles of wine.

MATERIALS

1 6-foot or 8-foot table and, depending on the surface of your table, a tablecloth

1 buffet platter, bowl, or other vessel for each menu element

1 candelabrum or 3 tall candlesticks

1 urn for wines on ice

1 dinner plate per person, plus 6 extra

1 platter to hold napkins and flatware

confetti

1. Set up your buffet table where it will be most convenient for serving and clearing without creating bottlenecks. Ideally, guests can approach the buffet table from both ends for the most fluid traffic flow. Unless you have a delicate surface or an unsightly table, you can eliminate a tablecloth. Toss confetti over the tabletop.

2. Early in the day, set the table with all the empty serving dishes to be used to be sure you have room for everything. Set them up in this order: stack dinner plates at one end, followed by side dishes and main meats. Napkin bundles are last. Use sticky notes to identify what each dish will hold until ready to serve.

3. During the party, remember to clear away the clutter. Used dishes, napkins, glasses, and serving dishes should be removed as soon as possible. It's better to have a slightly empty buffet than a messy one.

napkin roll

Make it easy for your guests to juggle plates full
of food by providing a platter full of utensils at the end of the buffet.
Wrap only the really necessary flatware inside a generous napkin
tied with a silver ribbon. I prefer thirsty, always-elegant white
linens. They look delicate but are a sturdy, bleachable fabric that
will look smart for many, many washings. Guests will thank you
if you serve bite-sized portions that eliminate the need for a knife,
a thoughtful gesture when a lap is also the table.

MATERIALS

1. Press napkin with spray starch for a crisp finish. Fold napkin
   into a square. Press folds. This step can be completed days
   before the party.
2. Pleat into 2½ inch panels to make an accordion fold. Top with
   flatware; tie with ribbon.

MAKES 1 BUNDLE

22-inch or 24-inch white
linen napkin

iron spray starch

flatware for one person

8-inch ribbon

caviar shooters

Buffet menus should include dishes that can be made ahead of time and that are easy to warm up or are meant to be served at room temperature. Roasted meats, cheesy soups, macaroni casseroles, vegetable lasagna, and rice salads are all excellent options. (A carb-heavy menu is a good thing on a night when people tend to drink more than usual.) I do love to break my own rules and surprise my guests with an unexpected spontaneous treat. Caviar shooters are simple to prepare but should be assembled right before serving them on a bed of crushed ice.

INGREDIENTS

1 clove garlic

1 cup thick Greek-style yogurt

16 tall shot glasses

2 ounces salmon roe caviar

1 box thin breadsticks

1. Peel and mince garlic; mix well with yogurt. (This can be done a day in advance.)
2. Place a tablespoon of yogurt into a tall shot glass. Top with teaspoon of salmon roe caviar.
3. Serve with breadsticks that can be used as spoons.

MAKES 16 SERVINGS

twelve
sweet grapes

New Year's Eve is a time to wish for a little luck for the new year. Many cultures have traditional favorites: In Sweden and Norway, a whole almond is hidden in dish of rice pudding, and whoever gets the nut will have a fortunate year. Greeks bake a round, sweet bread with a coin inside; the bread is cut at midnight, and the slices are distributed to guests in order of age. Italians serve honey-drenched balls of pasta dough fried and dusted with powdered sugar. In Germany, pancakes are considered so lucky that the batter is ladled into the skillet at midnight. In Spain, eating 12 grapes, one at a time, at the stroke of midnight promises good luck. I serve the grapes in a wine goblet with sorbet and a splash of spumante.

INGREDIENTS

12 grapes per serving

generous scoop of sorbet, either lemon or white grape

goblet

a splash of spumante

1. Clean grapes, remove from stems, and set aside until 15 minutes before midnight. (Grapes can be prepped early in the day.)
2. Scoop sorbet into each goblet and return to freezer until ready to serve. Stemless goblets are easy to stack in your freezer and can be prepared before your guests arrive.
3. Before midnight, remove goblets with sorbet from freezer, top with 12 grapes, and splash with champagne. Serve with a dessert spoon.

MAKES 1 SERVING

lucky lights

Flooding our home with candlelight is a beautiful and symbolic way to start the New Year. The bright, hopeful spirit of the flame is especially relevant on this night. Many cultures have ceremonies that use the moment of lighting a candle as a time to offer a blessing or to make a wish. As I run around our home fussing with last-minute details before guests arrive, lighting candles (a long-necked butane torch makes lighting 100 candles a breeze), I pause and wish my guests, my family, and the world peace.

Place rice and candles on platter. Light candles 10 minutes before guests are due to arrive.

MATERIALS

1 cup of dry rice

12 votive candles

14-inch platter, any shape

long-necked butane torch

lunar new year

One of my first dates with my husband was a trip to
Chinatown for the Lunar New Year celebrations. We held hands
to our ears as the big bangs of tiny firecrackers drum-rolled a
staged duel between 30-foot-long dragon puppets. The vibrant,
synchronized line of dancers warding off evil spirits is a highlight
of the nightly festivities that last two weeks between the new
moon and the full moon. Devotees ring in the new year—which
falls between January 21 and February 20—by cleaning their homes
from top to bottom, sweeping away the bad luck of last year.
Instead of spring cleaning for good luck, we invite friends to share
a meal that mixes all sorts of Asian symbolism and tastes in our
homespun wish for a year of good fortune, *Gong hay fat choy!*

dancing lanterns

Welcome guests with a squadron of gilded lanterns dressed in the most auspicious hues. Bright red, the color of happiness, is fittingly worn by brides on wedding days and is widely used to decorate because of its good-luck symbolism. Likewise, gold and orange are equally prized for prosperity. Bestow good fortune by decorating with lots of gold, red, and orange.

1. Extend lanterns to full size. Insert the metal frame that comes packaged with the lantern.
2. Working in a well-ventilated area, spritz small swatches of each lantern with gentle bursts of adhesive spray, rotating the lantern to be sure each panel receives a bit of spray.
3. Once the adhesive is tacky, apply one sheet of gold leaf to each sticky section. Rub gently to secure the metal tissue in place.
4. Knot the three lengths of ribbon together at one end and tie them to the metal strut at the bottom opening of each lantern.
5. Attach the nylon line to the metal strut at the top of the lantern with a slipknot.
6. Suspend the lanterns where they have plenty of clearance to swing— from trees in the yard, the balcony of a front porch. Or, because they are featherweight, simply thumbtack them to ceilings.

MAKES 1 LANTERN

MATERIALS

1 15-inch-square red paper lantern

adhesive spray

6 4-inch x 4-inch sheets gold leaf metal tissue

12 feet 2-inch-wide gold satin ribbon, cut into 3 4-foot ribbons

2 feet clear nylon fishing line

napkin detail

The right napkin instantly changes the look of any table—it's easy to transform any setting from fine to fabulous with the bold punctuation of the bright fabric. I dress up my classic white plates with lap-sized squares of a ruby and gold brocade embroidered with Chinese characters that I found while rummaging in a discount fabric shop. The best news is that you can make these napkins in less than 5 minutes—no sewing required.

MATERIALS

2 yards 45-inch-wide fabric

pinking shears

6 feet 1-inch-wide satin ribbon

vintage Chinese coins (or metal washers painted gold)

6 pairs chopsticks

1. Cut 6 22-inch squares from the 2 yards of fabric using pinking shears. The sawtooth blades cut a zigzag line and prevent fraying.
2. Cut the ribbon into 12-inch lengths.
3. Fold the fabric into a square.
4. Wrap the ribbon around the napkin and thread each end through the coin.
5. Insert the chopsticks between the napkin and ring.

MAKES 6 NAPKINS

origami parasols

Ever since I had my first tropical cocktail served with plump cherries and a sunny paper umbrella, I've loved the kitschy charm of cocktail parasols. I've anchored umbrellas to berries and set them afloat in fruity concoctions, even staked them atop cupcakes and saucers of sorbet. Although boxed packages of tiny umbrellas are widely available where cocktail supplies are sold, for the holiday I opt for a dressier version made from origami papers. These pretty papers come in a wide array of patterns and colors, so it's easy to find shades to complement this celebration. I station a batch of these mini-parasols at the bar in a tumbler filled with just enough rice to hold them in place.

MATERIALS

1. Using a drinking glass or compass, trace a 3¾-inch circle on the unprinted side of each sheet of origami paper.
2. Cut out the circle and cut a 2-inch line to the exact center of the circle.
3. Create a shallow cone with each circle of paper by overlapping 1 inch of the paper at the cut. Secure with a thin smear from a glue stick. Let dry.
4. Use a pair of flower clippers to cut the flat end of each skewer to a 5-inch length.
5. Spear the center of each parasol with the pointed end of the bamboo skewer. Turn the parasol upside down and apply a bead of rubber cement to the point where the stick meets the paper. Let dry.

MAKES 12 PARASOLS

drinking glass with 3¾-inch mouth, or a compass

12 4-inch squares of origami paper

scissors

glue stick

flower clippers

rubber cement

bamboo skewers

golden orange sake-tini

Many superstitions surround the Lunar New Year, but one common belief suggests that what happens on the first day of the new year portends the year to come. Just in case that's true, I say toast the year with an appropriately auspicious drink. The Golden Orange heralds a prosperous, fruitful year. Use Joss paper as coasters and garnish each drink with a dash of edible gold leaf for good fortune.

INGREDIENTS

martini glass

edible gold leaf
(see Resources)

small bowl

orange wedge

½ ounce orange-flavored
vodka

1 ounce orange liqueur or
Triple Sec

½ ounce sake

shot glass to measure

cocktail shaker

ice cubes

1. Chill the martini glass in your freezer.
2. Place a handful of gold leaf flakes in a small bowl or saucer. Set aside.
3. Just before mixing the martini, rub the rim of each glass with a wedge of orange. Roll the sticky rim in the gold leaf to coat lightly.
4. Pour vodka, Triple Sec, and sake into a cocktail shaker filled with ice. Shake for 10 seconds, strain, and pour into chilled martini glasses.

MAKES 1 COCKTAIL

take-out cartons

Ordering in Chinese food is almost a weekly event in our home. When we're working late, it's reassuring to know that a quick meal is a mere phone call away. I've always admired the practical packaging of the ubiquitous Chinese take-out carton, whose shape clearly says "yummy food inside." Empty cartons are available from many sources—container specialists, restaurant suppliers, and Asian importers—and lucky red boxes are not hard to find. The pint-sized cartons are handy for serving snacks like sesame pretzels, seaweed and rice crackers, shrimp and potato crackers, individual portions of noodles, stir-fried rice, or fortune cookies. All items for this idea can be easily found at Asian importers.

MATERIALS

1. Line each take-out container with two sheets of Joss paper. Fill each carton with your preferred dry snack.
2. Top bamboo tray with 4 sheets of Joss paper. Use to present cartons of snacks.

MAKES 4 CONTAINERS

4 pint-sized take-out containers

12 sheets Joss paper

4 assorted snacks

14-inch bamboo tray

bamboo steamers

The luckiest part of celebrating the Lunar New Year
is that it's oh-so-easy to create a feast for a crowd—you just need a
telephone. Pull out your favorite Chinese, Korean, Vietnamese,
Thai, and Japanese menus to order symbolic favorites: long
noodles, represent long life; dumplings, which are said to resemble
ancient gold ingots; and whole fish for prosperity. For a fuss-free
evening, empty take-out onto your favorite platters. I use my wok
to warm dumplings in inexpensive individual bamboo steamers
that go from kitchen to dinner plate in minutes. For 6 adults, order
6 selections of starters and 4 main courses, plus a noodle choice
and rice dish. Serve family style. Green tea ice cream and fortune
cookies make a delicious finish.

MATERIALS

6 dinner plates

6 sheets Joss paper

**6 5-inch bamboo steamers;
each set has 2 trays and a lid**

bunch of napa cabbage

18 ready-to-eat dumplings

wok

6 sets chopsticks

soy sauce

hot mustard

1. Top each plate with one sheet of Joss paper and one steamer tray.
   Set aside.

2. Separate 6 napa cabbage leaves from the bunch; rinse; line remaining
   6 trays with one leaf of napa cabbage. Top each leaf with three
   dumplings. Stack 6 trays and cover with one lid.

3. Simmer 1½ cups water in the wok. Position bamboo trays in center
   of wok, simmer for two minutes to warm leaves and reheat ready-to-
   eat take out dumplings.

4. Place one tray of dumplings atop the base tray on each plate, top
   with lids, chopsticks and serve immediately with soy sauce and hot
   mustard as condiments.

   MAKES 6 SERVINGS

sake tasting

The subtle flavors of sake is best appreciated in small sips from tiny mugs that fit in the palm of your hand. This mellow brew is made from fermented rice. Sake can be served chilled, like a fine vodka, or warm, like a mulled wine. Offer guests several selections of sake to taste—like filtered or unfiltered. To serve, I pour one from its own adorably buxom bottle, the other varieties from porcelain sake carafes. Distinguish the carafe with unfiltered sake by tying it with a red ribbon. Thimbles of wine are kept toasty by the radiant heat of river rocks warmed in my oven.

MATERIALS

1. Several days before the party, lightly spray river rocks with gold paint. Use a deep cardboard box for painting.
2. Trim all 4 sides of the brocade fabric with pinking shears. Line tray with fabric. Tuck the cut edges under the fabric to create a soft nest.
3. Preheat your oven to 250 degrees.
4. Place rocks on the middle shelf of the oven; heat for an hour or until very warm to the touch.
5. Warm the sake by submerging room-temperature bottles of it in the pot of hot (but not boiling) water for about 10 minutes.
6. Fill sake carafes with warm sake, place on tray, and surround with warm rocks and cups.

- 6 river rocks
- gold spray paint
- cardboard box
- 25-inch square of brocade fabric
- pinking shears
- 3 varieties of sake, available at liquor stores
- stockpot filled with a gallon of hot water
- sake cups and carafes
- 1 serving tray

joss paper vases

Ceremonial sheets of bamboo paper, known as Joss paper—burned to honor deities and ancestors—is detailed with gold to be more appealing to the "spirits." I find these equally popular with mere mortals for decorating—and they cost only pennies!

MATERIALS

1 flat-sided mixing glass, about 7 inches tall

4-inch swatch of adhesive-backed felt, available at craft stores

pencil

scissors

adhesive spray

2 sheets 6-inch x 8-inch Joss paper

glue stick

1. Place the bottom of the glass on the back of the felt. Trace the perimeter. Cut the circle. Set aside.

2. Spray the entire outer surface of the glass with an even coat of adhesive spray. Let it rest 30 seconds to maximize stickiness.

3. Attach the first sheet of Joss paper to the glass at a 45-degree angle so that the paper covers as much of the glass as possible. Rub gently into place. Rub the bottom corner to attach the paper smoothly to the bottom of the glass and turn the top corner into the mouth of the glass.

4. Repeat method with second sheet of paper, positioning the paper to cover the remaining sides. Rub the bottom corner to attach the paper smoothly to the bottom of the glass.

5. Use a glue stick to attach the top points of each sheet to the inner rim of the glass. Rub paper with your thumb to smooth the surface.

6. Peel the adhesive backing from the felt circle and stick it to the bottom of the glass. Rub with your thumb to secure.

7. Fill with water to display carnations and bamboo leaves, extra chopsticks, fortune cookies, or candles.

valentine's day

I do enjoy a day of romance. I remember our first Valentine's Day together. I was determined to have Brett think of me all day long, so I bought a bag of conversation hearts and spent the night before tucking individual hearts everywhere. I slipped a "lover boy" into his pants pocket, a "kiss me" in the fingertip of his glove, a "dear one" in his coat pocket, a "you're sweet" in his socks. One by one, I found places for dozens of candies—and they worked, just as planned. To make every day feel more romantic, the coziest place of your new nest should be the bedroom. A pile of soft pillows (at least four for each of you), a downy comforter, soft sheets, bedside lamps with low-wattage bulbs, candles, and music make a seductive recipe.

truffles

The year before we wed was spent apart. The distance between us was difficult to bear, but it forced us to put our feelings on paper. We treasured receiving letters full of love, longing, and details of our daily doings, and wrote to each other almost every day. Now we're lucky to spend most nights together, but we haven't lost our fondness for love notes. Take the time to spell out your feelings— it's a heartwarming gift to receive. Make sure your intentions are perfectly clear with a personal invitation to your Valentine. A hot-pink note card left on your lover's pillow is hard to miss, especially when it's madly stamped with a tiny pink heart. A pair of chocolates promises that it will be a sweet rendezvous.

INGREDIENTS

4 ounces dark chocolate

stainless steel bowl

¼ cup plus 1 tablespoon heavy cream, hot but not boiling

whisk

1 tablespoon unsalted butter at room temperature

melon baller

1½ ounces white chocolate

pink granulated sugar

20 mini paper cups

1. Melt the dark chocolate, stirring it in a stainless-steel bowl over barely simmering water.
2. Remove from heat and slowly whisk in heated cream. Once all the cream has been added, the chocolate mix, or ganache, should be smooth and hold the lines of the whisk.
3. Slowly whisk in the butter until it is incorporated. Refrigerate for 2 hours.
4. To make spheres, dip a small melon baller into hot water; tap off excess water; scoop into the chilled ganache.
5. Melt 3 ounces white chocolate over simmering water, stirring. Cool for 15 minutes. Dip each truffle into the melted chocolate. Coat with pink sugar. Serve each in a paper cup.

MAKES 20 TRUFFLES

sweetheart roses

Only one flower speaks the language of love with
certainty—the rose. This sultry flower, with so many silky petals,
opens to reveal a feathery heart with a gentle fragrance. In February,
roses are widely marketed as the only flower to give—the longer
the stem, the more prestigious the purchase. Valentine roses are
very expensive because of the demand. At this time of year, Brett
knows I prefer to receive almost any other flower (I'd rather splurge
on fine champagne) and save the romance of the rose for summer,
when it grows naturally and abundantly. But having a soft spot
for tradition—with a twist—I was happy to find teeny rose plants at
our local nursery with which to decorate our bedroom. The petite
blooms fit perfectly on our night tables and breakfast tray.

MATERIALS

1. Clip and trim individual stems of roses to fit in a shot glass. Allow
   about 4 stems per glass.
2. Fill glasses halfway with clear water. Add flowers.

MAKES 4 ARRANGEMENTS

2 4-inch pots of tiny roses,
available at nurseries and
groceries

scissors

4 tall shot glasses

mimosa

I can live without roses but not without champagne.
The bubbly brew sets just the right mood for romantic mornings
in bed. I like to mix sparkling wine with fresh juice, but ordinary orange
juice seems a bit too commonplace for Valentine's Day. Blood oranges,
with their crimson pulp, however, have an appropriately sexy tint to
blush the bubbles, and a rich flavor. Save the premium champagne
for the evening and opt for a reliable mid-range sparkling wine to mix
with juice. And remind him he's taken with red lipstick graffiti.

INGREDIENTS

3 blood oranges

hand juicer

small slotted spoon

pitcher

**bottle of well-chilled
sparkling wine**

2 flutes

1. Cut each orange in half, using a hand juicer to squeeze the pulp from
   each orange half into the pitcher. Use the slotted spoon to remove
   any seeds or unwanted pulp. Oranges can be juiced the night before
   and refrigerated.
2. Add sparkling wine to pitcher, 1 part juice to 2 parts wine.
3. Pour into flutes when ready to serve.

   MAKES 1 PITCHER

whipped cream
and berries

Fresh whipped cream seems like a luxurious indulgence, yet it's
one of the easiest treats to create. Share a bowl of bite-sized
raspberries—one of nature's perfect finger foods—and a generous
dollop of cream. A pefect pair for breakfast in bed.

INGREDIENTS

metal mixing bowl

hand mixer or metal whisk

**½ pint of heavy whipping
cream**

1 teaspoon of vanilla extract

2 tablespoon superfine sugar

½ pint fresh raspberries

dessert bowl

2 dessert spoons

1. Chill metal bowl and mixing blades or whisk in the freezer for at least
   30 minutes.
2. Pour ½ pint of whipped cream into the metal bowl and beat at a
   rapid rate until the cream becomes thick. It will double in volume and
   stand in small peaks when it coats the blades.
3. Add vanilla and sugar to taste. Cream can be made in advance; simply
   cover with plastic wrap and refrigerate until ready.
4. Rinse berries just before serving. Rest them briefly on a paper towel
   to absorb water, then fill bowl. Top with a large spoonful of whipped
   cream, and garnish the cream with one perfect berry.

MAKES 3 CUPS CREAM

butter hearts

I must admit that, in my career, I've been lucky to enjoy waking many mornings to the knock of room service in fine hotels. The la-di-da hotels never skimp on presentation—even the simplest meal of a tender croissant is served in grand style, with a pat of chilled butter and jam, a linen napkin, and a pot of fresh-brewed coffee. Spoil your mate with five-star treatment for pleasing results.

INGREDIENTS

1. Rinse knife under hot water, then slice butter into ¼–inch slices. Repeat as needed.
2. Use the cookie cutter to cut out a heart shape from each slice of butter, turning it on a diagonal to maximize surface area.
3. Place butter hearts between a folded sheet of wax paper, store in a plastic take-out container, and freeze 10 minutes to harden (or store until ready to use). These can be made days in advance.

chef's knife

½ stick unsalted butter, chilled

1-inch heart-shaped cookie cutter

wax paper

PRESSED COFFEE

To make coffee with a plunger pot, start with excellent, coarsely ground coffee, 1 rounded tablespoon per cup. Add boiling water to the pot, stir and steep for a few minutes, press, and serve. A mini stainless plunger pot makes quick foam from cream when pumped.

spring fling

Reliably, even after the most dismal winter, one day our garden turns green. Tiny flowers pop up, warmed by the sun. Birds chirp and bees hum, the sun shines longer, and my heart skips a happy beat. March 21 is the first full day of spring (and Brett's birthday!); when I was growing up, the cusp of the season was crowded with celebrations for Easter, Saint Patrick's Day, and birthdays. Grassy window boxes hung from window sills; baskets of pastel eggshells naturally tinted or gaily painted by children made their annual debut; leprechaun-sized pots of shamrocks sprouted like weeds; and buttercream blossoms on cakes were lip-smackingly delicious. Whichever holiday you celebrate, toast the season of renewal with a spring-hued brunch designed to show off Mother Nature's favorite color.

flower compote

Simply stated, green says spring. To celebrate the season I serve up a green centerpiece in my favorite crystal compote meant for desserts. To adapt this wide-mouthed vessel into a bon vivant vase, I used a grid of florist's tape to make it easier to position flowers. The tape sticks well to dry glass, disappearing under foliage and flowery heads.

MATERIALS

1. Line vessel with green banana leaves.
2. Create a grid pattern across the rim of a dry vase with strips of florist's tape. Stretch tape horizontally, rim to rim, at 2-inch intervals. Trim ends so that only a ¼-inch of tape overlaps the rim. Turn vase to vertically overlay additional tape. Wrap circumference of vase with 1 layer of tape to secure the ends of crisscrossed tapes in place.
3. Add water to halfway point.
4. Trim stems of flowers to fit the height of the vase so that the heads of the flowers rest just above the rim. Insert stems into the grid, spacing the stems so the blooms fully cover the top of the vase.
5. Insert stems of ferns randomly to create a fuzzy fringe.

10-inch-wide-mouth vessel

2 banana leaves or other long, wide leaves

spool of ¼-inch florist's tape, clear or green

florist's knife or scissors

15 stems of green chrysanthemums; each stem has about a dozen flowers

6 stems of ferns

flower cubes

As the weather warms I yearn for chilled drinks. I always store a few flutes and tumblers in the freezer—frosty glasses make the first sips of any drink more delicious. But for parties, decorative ice cubes make a real splash. Start with distilled water or just-boiled water to make the clearest ice cubes (cubes made with tap water have mineral content and air bubbles that make cubes appear cloudy). Make a batch of cubes a couple of days before your party, pop from ice trays, and store in freezer bags until needed. Brew green tea and blend with equal parts limeade for a refreshing spring mix, serve over flower cubes.

MATERIALS

fresh flower blossoms,
1 per cube

mint leaves

ice cube tray

distilled or boiled water

plastic tubs or plastic
storage bags

1. Rinse flowers and mint leaves. Let dry, trim from stems, and discard any bruised or damaged foliage.
2. Fill ice cube trays ⅓ full with distilled or boiled water.
3. Freeze for about an hour. Remove, place one flower or mint leaf in each cube, top with water. Freeze until hard.
4. Rinse bottom of tray with warm water to remove cubes from trays. Store in plastic tubs or plastic storage bags in the freezer until ready to use.

HOMEMADE COASTERS
Use a 3-inch circle punch to cut out paper circles from cover-weight paper, and a rubber stamp to decorate the coaster with your monogram.

canned daisies

Pantries are full of all sorts of necessary staples, and the basic tin can might be the most versatile. Sturdy and trim, metal cans can be recycled for many uses. Empty 32- and 48-ounce vessels make handy watertight vases. I especially love cans that have ribbed detailing, a common pottery pattern that I find appealing when I'm using the cans to hold flowers.

MATERIALS

1. Use pliers to flatten any sharp edges inside the tin can.
2. Fill halfway with water; add favorite flowers.
3. Tie 2 strands of long grass around the center of the can; knot into place.

pliers

tin can (remove label, wash well)

water

bunch of flowers

2 15-inch strands of grass or raffia

simple place mat

Synthetic suede, best known by the trademarked name Ultrasuede, is a remarkable fabric. Plush and machine washable, it's an easy-to-care-for fabric that sports an elegant look. The material is widely used commercially for upholstery and clothing because of its durability and fashion sense; plus, it comes in dozens of colors, enough to excite any designer. To make a placemat, simply cut the fabric to fit your needs—no sewing, no seaming—and it's ready to use. For a stylishly simple place card, cut a circle that fits inside the rim of your plate. I use a rubber stamp to add a grassy detail and a green marker to pen our guests' names.

MATERIALS

fabric chalk

yardstick

1 yard synthetic suede fabric, 54 inches wide

scissors

exacto knife or craft knife

1. Use chalk and yardstick to mark out 12-inch x 18-inch rectangles on the fabric.
2. Use sharp scissors to cut out each rectangle.
3. Use chalk to trace a pair of 2-inch-long parallel lines, 1 inch apart, 1 inch from the left margin and midway between the top and the bottom of the 12-inch side.
4. Cut along the pair of chalk lines with an exacto knife.
5. When setting the table, slip the knife and fork through the slit to anchor the flatware in place.

MAKES 9 PLACE MATS

egg salad

More eggs are sold before Easter than at any other time of year. Fittingly, the week after is National Egg Salad Week. Eggs are sold in cartons to protect them while shipping and—because they have a porous skin—to avoid odors in the refrigerator. This sturdy carton is also a great way to serve eggs salad in eggshell cups. Simple wood paddles make perfect spoons for each eggshell.

INGREDIENTS

1. Place 6 eggs in a saucepan that allows the eggs just enough space to lie together. Cover with 1 inch of room-temperature water. Bring to a boil, lower heat to a simmer, and cook for 7 minutes. Remove eggs from water and submerge in large bowl of very cold water to chill.

2. Crack open the dozen uncooked eggs, using a knife to gently tap open the top end of the shell. You'll want to preserve ⅔ of the shell intact. Pour out the egg contents and set aside. (If lightly beaten together first, the eggs can be frozen in an airtight container for later use.)

3. Place the empty shells in a stockpot water bath and bring to a simmer. Remove from heat, cool, and clean. Set aside.

4. To crack cooked eggs, tap each against the counter and roll it under the palm of your hand to crackle the skin. Peel and discard shells.

5. Place cooked eggs in a large mixing bowl. Use a knife or *mezzaluna* to dice them, add ¼ cup of mayonnaise and diced celery, and mix well with a fork. Flavor with salt, pepper, and mustard to taste. Cover with plastic wrap and refrigerate until serving.

6. When ready to serve, remove the carton top and discard. Spoon egg salad into each eggshell, top with a ½ teaspoon of caviar, and nest in the carton with a spoon to serve.

MAKES 12 SERVINGS

18 eggs

saucepan to hold 6 eggs

mixing bowl

knife or *mezzaluna*

stockpot

¼ cup mayonnaise

2 stalks celery, finely diced

salt and pepper to taste

favorite mustard

plastic wrap

1 egg carton

1 ounce kelp caviar

12 wood spoons

mini-cupcakes

Spring flings should offer flowery menus that celebrate the season. Baskets of fresh herbs promise flavor and serve as picturesque garnishes. The season's first offerings—asparagus, rhubarb, and peas—spark my imagination; they make delicious ingredients for soups, salads, and desserts. The perfect finish for this seasonal supper? Tiny two-bite cupcakes iced with buttercream. A very tasty cake is available at my local grocer and I don't feel one bit guilty serving store-bought sweets. Entertaining well doesn't mean spending hours in the kitchen. The key is knowing where to find all the right, easy, delicious elements and how to present them. Map out the best purveyors in your area and get to know their specialties. It's how you put the details together that creates a distinctive event.

MATERIALS

12 small pansies, available from farmers markets and nurseries

paper towel

circle cutter

½ yard decorative paper

scissors

12 mini cupcakes, available at grocers

3 dinner plates

1. Wash pansies with water, trim blossoms from stems, and dry on paper towel.
2. Use a circle cutter to cut a 6-inch circle from decorative paper. Cut out shapes. Look for circle cutters at craft stores for a smooth cut.
3. Place one paper disc on each plate.
4. Top each cupcake with a pansy. Serve 6 cupcakes per plate for guests to share.

   MAKES 3 PLATES

earth day

Long before the easy information-sharing opportunities of the Internet were available, determined conservationists started a grassroots movement to establish Earth Day, on April 22, 1970. Their seeds of hope and protest clearly took root and had an impact on our communities. Once-dormant rivers have come back to life, many habitats are now protected, renewable sources of energy promoted, recycling enforced, air-quality controls and environmental guidelines established. But there remains so much more to do as natural habitats dwindle and communities compete for resources that humanity consumes voraciously. Invite friends to a celebration that's also a call to action. Pledge to reuse and recycle materials whenever possible; aim to use sustainable and biodegradable resources; eat locally and plant green—all important ways to protect the earth.

burlap napkins

Jute fibers, woven from a quick-growing plant, are strong and supple, and yield two of the world's most utilitarian fabrics, burlap and canvas. These hardworking natural fibers are a gardener's favorite. They're used most often for bagging and screening, but they can also lend your table a stylish sensibility. Go natural with jute and other sustainable plants, like teak and bamboo, which are now crafted into eco-conscious tableware. Their cultivation promotes healthy indigenous communities around the world, an earth-friendly policy.

MATERIALS

1. Use pinking shears to cut out 18-inch squares from burlap.
2. Use pinking shears to cut a dozen ½-inch strips 10 inches long from remnant canvas.
3. Fold the burlap into a square. Rest flatware in the center; wrap and knot with 1 canvas tie.

MAKES 12 NAPKINS

pinking shears

2 yards of 54-inch-wide burlap

remnant canvas strips, about 20 square inches

cardboard
coasters

Reuse and recycle. The more we find a way to minimize our debris, the more we help our planet. Wine bottles can be turned into vases, old towels into polishing cloths, shredded plastic bags make super stuffing for doggie lounge pillows, tin cans turn into vases, burlap into napkins. With a little thought, there are ways to repurpose so many things. Cardboard packaging inserts are sturdy and absorbent; when they are cut to size and decorated with a floral rubber stamp to suit the occasion, they make ideal coasters.

MATERIALS

2 sheets 11-inch x 8-inch cardboard

paper cutter

daisy print rubber stamp

green ink pad

green marker

1. Cut the cardboard sheet into 3½-inch squares. Each sheet will make 6 squares.
2. Detail cards with the rubber stamp. Create a repeating wallpaper pattern by overlapping the same stamp.
3. Use the marker to edge the 4 sides of the coasters.

MAKES 12 COASTERS

personal plants

When I was in elementary school, we planted trees in
the schoolyard to commemorate Arbor Day, first celebrated in
Nebraska in 1872. We dug holes for scrawny saplings, watered them
well, and sang a song. Years later I was proud to see these plantings
mature into shade trees that now brought relief to a new generation
of students. More than 100 years ago, and a century before concerns
of global warming, there was an emerging awareness that the
greening of our communities was an important objective. Encourage
your guests to embrace and sustain the green spirit by offering
small plants in peat pots that can be planted as is.

MATERIALS

12 small green plants

12 2-inch peat pots

12 wood coffee stirrers

marker

1. Transplant small plants into a peat pot. Press the soil and plant into
   each pot with your fingertips.
2. Use a marker to letter coffee stirrers with your guests' names; insert
   vertically into pot like a garden stake.
   MAKES 12 POTTED PLANTS

wine bottle vases

The lean, elegant silhouette of a wine bottle lends itself to a second life as a bud vase. It's shaped to hold a well of liquid and its narrow neck makes it a superior vessel for long-stemmed flowers and foliage. Fill the bottles with shoots of ivy; these hardy plants are easy to root and, once established, make a natural sun shade. Let your centerpieces inspire conservation-minded conversation—remind everyone that homes with well-placed shrubs and leafy vine cover help reduce energy costs by shading the building. It pays to go green.

MATERIALS

3 used wine bottles

bottle brush

adhesive solvent

water

3 10-inch ivy shoots

1. Clean used wine bottles with bottle brush. Use adhesive solvent to remove any label remants.
2. Fill each bottle halfway with water. Remove several leaves from the end of the ivy stems to easily insert into the bottles. Be sure at least 2 inches of the root end of the stem is submerged in water.

MAKES 3 ARRANGEMENTS

crudités

Celebrate spring and the bounty of the earth with a medley of seasonal vegetables. Instead of presenting guests with mountains of crunchy vegetables to be picked through, I prefer to set up personal portions in shot glasses or glass votive holders, and serve each with a tablespoon of dipping sauce. Each glass holds a mini-salad that's symbolic of a petite garden, meant to remind us that Mother Earth can sustain us if we treat her well.

INGREDIENTS

12 shot glasses or votive holders

2 bunches baby bok choy

2 hearts of celery

8 ounces of green beans

1 bunch of skinny asparagus

1 bunch of baby carrots

1 seedless cucumber

paper towel

1 clove garlic

1 cup thick Greek-style plain yogurt

½ lemon, juiced

ground pepper

1. Place clean glasses in the refrigerator to chill.
2. Separate leaves of bok choy and stalks of celery; rinse well.
3. Clean green beans and asparagus, and slice each in half diagonally. Blanch beans for 4 minutes and asparagus for 2 minutes in simmering water. Rinse in cool water.
4. Peel carrots; slice in half vertically.
5. Peel cucumber so that thin slivers of skin remain. Cut into 2 4-inch-long sections and cut each into ½-inch thick strips.
6. Cover all prepared veggies with a damp paper towel, and crisp in the refrigerator until serving time.
7. Crush garlic and mix with yogurt, lemon juice, and pepper to taste.
8. Spoon yogurt into shot glass. Fill with mix of vegetables and serve.

MAKES 12 SERVINGS

solar tea

Energy-efficient and delicious, tea on ice is a bracing thirst quencher. Fill glass vessels with water and use the sun's rays to brew a hearty batch of teas. Serve in vintage milk bottles or mason jars with simple syrup for an old-fashioned charm.

1. Fill 3 quart bottles with water; add 3 tea bags to each bottle. Cover with lids or plastic wrap; let sit in full sun for an hour to steep. Remove tea bags. Chill tea in refrigerator.

2. To prepare simple syrup, bring 2 cups of water to a boil; mix in sugar and dissolve. Cool. Pour into ½-quart bottle.

3. Add sliced lemons to lemon tea, sprigs of mint to black tea, and berries to fruit tea. Cover with lids or cut a 6-inch swatch of cheesecloth to cover mouths of bottles; secure with wired twine.

4. Serve with simple syrup and tall glasses of ice.

MAKE 3 QUARTS TEA

INGREDIENTS

3 quart-sized water bottles or mason jars for 3 kinds of tea

1 gallon plus 2 cups pure water

9 tea bags of assorted teas— lemon, black, fruit flavors are favorites

1 ½-quart bottle

2 cups superfine sugar

1 lemon, thinly sliced

3 mint stems, rinsed

1 cup raspberries

1 foot cheesecloth

scissors

wired twine

stone cairn

Walking on the beach, I find smooth, flat stones that Brett finds ideal for skipping. I like to hold them in my hand, wondering how long it's taken to become the perfect size that fits in the palm of my hand. Like ancients who'd stack stones into cairns to mark special places, once home I fill small bowls and make simple sculptures. I find the natural decor peaceful. Hold a sliver of earth in your hand and consider the eons it took to create a habitable world. Reflect on the implications of our existence and how we can affect our world in a positive way. Imagine the possibilities and do what you can to live consciously.

MATERIALS

Wash stones, stack or pile on a tray, serving dish, or accent plate.

flat stones, found at the beach, forest, or garden center

serving platter

cinco de mayo

Get out the maracas, and rumba! Historically, May 5 commemorates a Mexican battle fought in 1862, but in recent years Cinco de Mayo has become an appreciation day for Latinos and lovers of Latinos. My mother was born in Guatemala, Mexico's neighbor. Mom moved to the United States when she was merely 20 and fell in love with my Irish dad. They proceeded to have 12 children in the next 14 years. Even though she was busy weaning babes and learning American ways she taught me to appreciate my roots. She introduced me to real corn tortillas and my favorite, chiles rellenos, Mama Lina style. She'd croon Latin love songs to lull us to sleep and do housework to a marimba beat. If I learned anything from Mom's Spanglish, it was to celebrate life and family ties.

chelada

Cold beer is *muy importante* for any fiesta. It's best to chill bottles on their side in a bed of ice to avoid a hot neck, and then prop them up just before serving. To quick-chill a warm neck, turn the beer upside down into the ice for a couple of minutes. Slice wedges of lemons and limes to squeeze into bottle necks for a fresh zest. Leave gringo beers for another day, and pick up some widely available Mexican *cervezas*. For a refreshing beer spritzer, serve over crushed ice to make a *chelada*.

INGREDIENTS

1 lime to juice

1 lime to slice

hand juicer

½ cup crushed ice

sea salt

glass

jigger

beer

1. Roll a lime under the palm of your hand against the counter top to break up membranes and release its juice. Slice in half and use the hand juicer to ream the juice from the fruit. Set aside.
2. Slice the lime in ¼-inch discs. Cut a disc in half and slice a notch along one of the membranes so the slice can perch on the glass rim as a sidecar.
3. Rub the rim of a tall glass with one of the lime slices, then dip the rim in sea salt to lightly coat. Fill the glass with crushed ice. Top with your favorite beer, ½ jigger of lime juice, and a grind of sea salt.

MAKES 1 SERVING

margarita

I remember our first great margarita. On a summer road trip to Southern California, stunned by the desert heat, we stumbled into a dark oasis called ¡Viva Mexico! We spent the afternoon in a cozy booth, delighted at our luck and quenching our thirst with just the right blend of sweet, sour, and ice. The blue agave plant, native to Tequila, Mexico, is the main ingredient. Tequila has three basic distinctions: *Joven* (unaged) is available as *oro* (gold) and *blanco* (white) or *plata* (silver) are best for mixing. *Reposado* (rested) is aged from 2 months to a year; and *Añejo* (old) is aged between 1 year and 3 years. (Extra *añejo* is aged over 3 years). The best tequilla is 100 percent blue agave.

INGREDIENTS

1. Cut lime in half, squeeze juice in a shaker. Add tequila, Triple Sec, sugar, and ice. Cover, shake well for 10 seconds.
2. Rub the flesh of the lime around the rim of each glass to make sticky.
3. Place salt in a saucer and rotate the sticky rim of the glass in the salt to lightly coat.
4. Pour ice and well-mixed combination into each glass. If you prefer to serve straight, strain to remove the cubes.
5. Garnish each drink with several thin slices of Key lime and one flower.

MAKES 2 MARGARITAS

2 ounces fresh lime juice (about one juicy lime)

shaker

4 ounces tequila

2 ounces Triple Sec or premium orange liqueur, like Cointreau

1 tablespoon superfine sugar

2 cups ice

¼ cup kosher salt

saucer

2 glasses

1 finely sliced Key lime

2 edible flowers, like orchids

floating flowers

Fresh flower mosaics are a ceremonial tradition
in Latin America. The bright petals are arranged in vivid patterns
through the streets for important religious holidays. Known as
alfombras, or "carpets," they are lush and vibrant like a woven oriental
rug. Inspired by their beauty, I've made *alfombras* for wedding aisles
and floated flowers in simple glass bowls for watery tapestries
that are also an affordable centerpiece. Make your own water garden
with a handful of your favorite flowers and almost any wide bowl.

MATERIALS

14-inch glass bowl

4 cups water

12 flower heads

flower clippers

1. Add 1 inch water to glass bowl.
2. Remove stems from flower heads, float in bowl. Pull apart 1 or 2
   flowers to scatter loose petals in the water.

   MAKES 1 CENTERPIECE

paper flowers

If you go bright, you can't go wrong. Fiesta-worthy, hot colors that look vibrant even in bright sunlight are the only tones to consider. For the table, look for brightly woven cotton textiles to use as a tablecloth; imported fabrics are affordable and easy to find. Loyalists may want to decorate with red, green, and white, the colors of the Mexican flag, but I choose the broader spectrum of a Guatemalan rainbow. Napkins are actually thirsty dish towels, and instead of a napkin ring, I simply fold a sheet of tissue into paper flowers. ¡Olé!

MATERIALS

1. Cut the sheet of tissue paper into 4-inch by 8-inch pieces.
2. Stack 2 sheets of tissue to make each flower. Fold the pair of sheets to make a square. Use your fingers to press the fold.
3. Beginning at the fold, pleat the entire square of tissue into 1/8-inch accordion folds.
4. Twist 1 end of the wire around the center point of the pleated paper.
5. Use scissors to cut round corners at each end of the folded paper.
6. Use your thumbs to fan out a half of the flower. Gently pull each layer apart to create a row of petals. Repeat on other side.
7. Fold napkin and wrap the wire stem around its center.

MAKES 8 FLOWERS

1 sheet 20-inch by 30-inch tissue paper

2 yards 26-gauge paper-covered wire, available in florist's supply shops, cut into 8-inch lengths

scissors

salsa-tinis

The martini glass is a versatile vessel, serving cocktails
and treats with equal aplomb. The wide mouth makes a beautiful
bowl, perfect for offering tasting-sized portions. The broad rim
of the glass makes it easily stackable. Cluster 8 stems together and
top with another 3 and a single glass for a third tier—an acrobatic
presentation that spells fun, and gives you license to rename anything
you serve in it with the last syllable -tini. For a modified Latin beat
I like to serve salsa salad. The main ingredient is tomato, a fruit native
to South America, and possibly the most valuable treasure found
by the conquistadors. This fresh salad seasoned with oil, lemon, salt
and pepper, is a versatile accompaniment to fish, meat, or beans.

INGREDIENTS

2 cups grape tomatoes, sliced
in threes

coarse salt and pepper to taste

1 long seedless cucumber,
peeled and sliced thin

juice of 1½ limes

3 small white onions, peeled,
finely sliced

30 small leaves mint or cilantro

2 tablespoons extra-virgin
olive oil

12 martini glasses

12 cocktail forks

1. Toss tomatoes with coarse salt—3 or 4 grinds of the salt mill
   should do.
2. Toss cucumber slices with a grind of salt, pepper, and the juice
   of one lime.
3. After salted cucumber and tomatoes rest for 5 minutes,
   toss together with onions, mint or cilantro, olive oil, and the
   remaining lime juice.
4. Fill each martini glass halfway with salad. Stack and serve with
   cocktail forks.

   MAKES 12 SERVINGS

candles
in the trees

The best celebrations last long into the night
(that's why an afternoon siesta before the festivities begin is a good
idea). To keep the mood fiesta-ful, decorate with dozens of candles.
Votives in brightly colored glasses are lovely for tables, but I like
to fill the trees with lights, too. Twine tote bags, made to carry wine
bottles, are very sturdy pouches that make excellent candle sconces.
The sacks are available in bright colors to match the celebration, but
it would be easy to dye natural fibers in vibrant tones.

MATERIALS

6 large drinking glasses

6 twine totes

6 cups of water

6 2-inch floating candles

long-necked butane torch

1. Insert glass into twine tote. Fill glass with 1 cup of water;
    float candle.
2. Hang totes just above eye level among the lower branches of
    the trees in your garden. Cluster candles in groups of 3 and 5
    to brighten up the yard. Use a long-necked butane torch to
    make illuminating each easy.

    MAKES 6 HANGING CANDLES

flag day

Summer's lazy, sunny season begins with a pair of patriotic holidays: Memorial Day and the Fourth of July. Celebrated with flag-waving on Main Street, high-stepping brass bands, grills smoldering with fat burgers and hot dogs, fireworks illuminating faces sticky with cotton candy—all of these offer a comforting blanket of tradition woven red, white, and blue. Consider it your patriotic duty to have a party. Orchestrate your celebration around all-American crowd pleasers: Listen to rock and roll, brassy New Orleans–style jazz, and John Philip Sousa; play baseball, football, or volleyball; take a picnic to the beach, the park, or your backyard; serve surf and turf; take a nap in a hammock and swoon under the stars; and toast the many who've made sacrifices so that we can continue to enjoy the simple pleasures we consider a constitutional right.

hydrangea
centerpiece

Massive fluffy balls of hydrangea erupt with a bang. When nature's fireworks appear, you know summer's in full bloom. Besides the showy colors, the most fabulous thing about hydrangeas is the size of each flower head—a few stems go a long way. I love using them to create simple centerpieces. For a shipshape arrangement, fill a cobalt glass pitcher laced up with plain clothesline and anchored with a basic square knot. Beach in a small mound of sand for a nautical note.

MATERIALS

pitcher

1 yard of clothesline

fresh water

4 stems hydrangea

flower clippers

4 cups sand

1. Wrap neck of pitcher with coil of clothesline; tie off the 2 ends of the line with a square knot. To make a square knot, cross the left end of the line over the right to make an *X*, then tuck the left line under and around the opposite line—just like tying a shoelace. Pull each end of the line to make the knot tight. Then cross the right end of the line over the left to make a reverse *X*, repeat the shoelace knot, and pull ends to tighten.

2. Fill half of the pitcher with clear, tepid water.

3. Trim any excess or damaged foliage from each hydrangea stem. Use flower clippers to trim the end of the stem to fit your pitcher. Flower heads should rest just above the mouth of the pitcher. Make a sharp, slanted cut across the base of the stem, then cut a 1-inch perpendicular slice into the stem for maximum water absorption. Place stems in the pitcher and fluff the flower heads.

4. Pour sand directly onto your tabletop to create a shallow mound, and center the pitcher in the sand. Add a shell, if desired.

MAKES 1 CENTERPIECE

serving tray

What's more patriotic than reusing and recycling?
It's another way to preserve our natural national resources. The same white frame I used for a New Year's tray makes a snappy base when lined with red, white, and blue ribbons. To quench the thirst of flag-wavers, serve cranberry juice on ice and white grape juice that's been tinted blue with a drop of food coloring.

1. Cut ribbon into 11-inch lengths. Group by color; set aside.

2. Spray glass cleaner directly on a paper towel and wipe the panes clean. (To remove any lint that might remain, a ball of crumpled newspaper may be more effective against static than the paper towel.)

3. Turn the frame upside down. Remove any hardware from the back of the frame so the tray will lie flat on a tabletop. Insert 1 pane of glass into the frame. Alternating colors, place ribbons in a row pattern to fill the frame. Top with the second pane of glass.

4. Use the putty knife to insert two glazing or framing points into each side of the frame to hold the glass securely in place. Position each point 2 inches from each corner; the flat side of the point should rest directly on the glass with the tip pointed toward the frame. The notch of the points will fit against the blade of the knife—simply push the point into the wood.

MATERIALS

scissors

2½ yards each ½-inch-wide red, white, and blue grosgrain ribbon

glass cleaning solution

paper towels or newspaper

white wood frame with 11-inch x 14-inch opening

11-inch x 14-inch panes of precut glass

1-inch putty knife

8 glazing points

blue table

Eating outdoors is a summer rite. Build a simple table to lounge around with one sheet of wood—your hardware store can do all the cutting—paint it glossy, watery blue, and use sawhorses for legs. Drape a cotton cloth over the legs for a nautical wave and cut a hole in the center of the tabletop for the pole of a beach umbrella.

MATERIALS

1 4-foot x 8-foot ¾-inch MDF (medium density fiberboard), available at lumberyards

wood glue

36 2-inch drywall screws

8 ½-inch drywall screws

drill with screwdriver bit and pilot hole bit

6 clamps for 4-inch-wide board

wood filler

2-inch hole saw bit

medium sandpaper

1 gallon wood primer

3-inch paintbrush

1 quart royal blue high-gloss enamel

foam roller pad

painting tray

1 pair 26-inch-long sawhorses

1. Have the lumberyard cut MDF sheet into 1 32-inch-by-8-foot section and 4 8-foot-by-3-inch boards. Then have them cut 2 of the narrow boards into 4 sections, each 30½-inch by 3-inch.

2. Construct an open box with wood glue to attach the 2 long boards to the 2 short boards. This box will become the apron around the the table. Connect each corner with 2 2-inch screws using drill bits.

3. Working atop a pair of sawhorses, mount the frame with a bead of wood glue to the 32-inch wide board; it will look like a large tray. Clamp in place. Let dry overnight. Flip tabletop and drill pilot holes from the top of the table through the apron every 12 inches along the perimeter. Attach with 2-inch drywall screws. Use the drill bit to install the screw just below the wood surface. Fill with wood filler. Flip tabletop once again to attach two support struts with the 30 ½-inch wood boards, space to create 3 equal sections. Secure in place to the apron with ½-inch drywall screws. When complete use the hole bit to cut a 2-inch circle through the center of the table.

4. Smooth any rough edges with sandpaper. Use a paintbrush to cover with 3 coats primer. Let dry thoroughly between each coat. When dry, apply high-gloss enamel paint with roller pad.

5. Position sawhorses 4 feet apart and parallel. Top with cloth and table.

MAKES 1 TABLETOP

mini-aquariums

Neptune's world is a beautiful environment; all sand
and shells, it makes a mesmerizing centerpiece. Shrink the ocean
to a globe that you can hold in the palm of your hand by filling
a squadron of goblets with handfuls of sand and a few shells
for an underworldly display. Line up goblets across your tabletop
(or mantel or window sill) to give everyone a beachy view.

MATERIALS

Pour ½ cup of sand into each goblet; cover with 1 cup water. When the
water settles, drop 3 shells in each glass.

MAKES 12 MINI-AQUARIUMS

**6 cups fine white sand,
available at aquarium
suppliers**

12 goblets

12 cups water

36 mixed shells

napkin knots

I've found that thirsty budget-priced kitchen towels make great lap linens. They have generous proportions, often come in simple colors like nautical blue with white stripes, and launder easily. Local sailors shop at a marine center that stocks everything they need to keep their ships in shape, and there I found a batch of cotton fisherman's bracelets (so named because they were worn to wipe deckhand brows) that are also sold as friendship bracelets, meant to be worn all summer long. These sturdy knots make ideal napkin rings for guests to keep as a token of our affection.

MATERIALS

10-inch by 20-inch cotton dish towel

fisherman's bracelet

starfish

1. Fold towel in half lengthwise and fold again widthwise. Fold in a triple accordion pleat.
2. Encircle with fisherman's bracelet. Rest on dinner plate with starfish tucked into bracelet.

MAKES 1 NAPKIN BUNDLE

stuffed shrimp

The coastal waters offer a cooling respite and a delicious repast. A bed of sea glass makes a beachy nest for scallop shells, perfect shallow bowls for summery appetizers.

1. Simmer water in large pan with sliced lemon, onions, garlic, and peppercorns. Poach shrimps for 3 minutes. Remove from heat; cool, rinse, and peel. Remove the entire shell but leave the fantail for presentation. Use a paring knife to make a thin cut along the back spine toward the tail to devein. Rinse. Make another shallow cut in the belly of the shrimp to butterfly the shrimp. Chill in the refrigerator.

2. Prepare crabmeat. In a large bowl, separate flakes lightly with a fork and toss with mayonnaise, ground pepper, and lemon juice. Chill in the refrigerator.

3. When ready to serve, spread 1 cup of sea glass and 3 scallop shells on each plate.

4. Spread 1 tablespoon wakame seaweed in each scallop shell. To season seaweed, toss with equal parts sesame oil and rice vinegar.

5. Top seaweed with 1 shrimp, and fill with a teaspoon of crabmeat. Garnish with ⅓ teaspoon of caviar.

MAKES 8 SERVINGS

4 cups water

1 lemon, sliced thin

1 small onion, sliced thin

10 peppercorns

1 pound large shrimp, at least 24 count

paring knife

1 clove garlic, sliced thin

⅔ pound lump crabmeat

2 tablespoon mayonnaise

ground pepper to taste

juice of ½ lemon

½ pound wakame seaweed salad, available at Asian specialty markets

1 tablespoon sesame oil

1 tablespoon rice vinegar

8 cups sea glass

24 scallop shells

8 plates

2 ounces whitefish caviar

galvanized
ice bucket

Cold beverages are the refreshment of choice on a hot day. To keep drinks both handy and frosty, I look no further than my hardware store, which is stocked with practical provisions that are durable and multifunctional. Galvanized buckets have a hardy homestead appeal that feels appropriate on a deck, a beach, or at a picnic.

MATERIALS

8-quart galvanized bucket

3 pounds ice cubes

2 quarts water

3 bottles of favorite water or beverage

For a perfect chill, fill bucket with ⅓ each of ice and cool water and submerge bottles up to their shoulders to chill. As ice melts, simply pour out excess water and replenish with more ice. Rest bucket in the shade for best results.

MAKES 1 COOLER

floating candles

When the long summer days slide into twilight, it's time to light candles. Outdoor candles need protection from the wind. I like to use large bubble bowls as hurricanes. The clear, simple shape is a versatile blank canvas, ready to be filled with your ideas. For a serene, summery tableau, water is the perfect solution: practically free, easy to work with, and naturally elegant (and if you don't have a water view, you'll feel like you do). A base of sea glass makes a sparkling beach for the candlelight; it's fun to collect, but you can buy a bucket of beach glass, tumbled to remove sharp points as the sea would, at a craft store. Just rinse in a colander to reuse at your next summer gathering.

MATERIALS

1. Place sea glass in the bottom of the bubble bowl.
2. Fill ⅓ of the bowl with clear water.
3. Float candles in the bowl; light when ready.

MAKES 1 HURRICANE

16-inch bubble bowl

2 cups blue sea glass, available at craft shops

2 quarts water

3 3-inch blue floating candles

long-necked butane torch

labor day

The calendar says it's not so, but for most of us, Labor Day weekend marks the end of summer. For me, it's the anniversary of the night that changed my life. Although I was fully prepared for a college game plan that included dating all sorts of clever men, fate had a different plan. I met my husband my first night on campus, Labor Day weekend. Since then, Labor Day celebrations are an anniversary party for us—not of the formal sort, with a night of dressing up as we do on our wedding anniversary, but one that echoes the same easy way we met. The long, lazy weekend allows us to indulge in our favorite sports of lounging and loving, cooking and chatting, sunning and stargazing.

tree trunk trivets

Weathered textures in simple compositions are my favorite compositions to put together. I love to use local harvests, along with found objects and treasures from my walks—nothing fancy, but together, tree stumps, clay pots, and sunny flowers make a striking tableau. Sunflowers take all summer to grow fat and sunny; by Labor Day, the farmers' fields of Van Gogh's favorite are leggy and precocious, begging to be cut and placed into pots. When our old crabapple tree had to be cut down, I had thick rings cut in different heights to make perfect pedestals and trivets. Examine and admire the natural elements around you, and before something is discarded, contemplate its reusability. Finding a way to make the most of everything is the earth-friendly way to live.

MATERIALS

Cut 2 each 2-inch-, 3-inch-, and 4-inch-wide cross-sections from the log to make trivets. Use the trivets as pedestals for pots of flowers. To set a buffet, stagger the placement and mix the heights of the pedestals for a more dramatic display. Precut log rings can often be found at garden centers.

MAKES 6 TRIVETS

2-foot-long 8-inch-wide log with bark

chain saw

monogram tray

To mark our anniversary, I decorate with our shared initial. I branded a rough wood frame with our letter before filling the frame with sunflower petals to make a sunny platter for serving drinks.

4 large sunflowers

branding iron

weathered wood frame with 11-inch x 14-inch opening

11-inch x 14-inch panes of precut glass

paper towels or newspaper

glass-cleaning solution

1-inch putty knife

8 glazing points, available in framing supply shops

1. With gentle tugs, remove petals from sunflower heads. Set aside.

2. Heat one burner on stove top to high setting. Place the brand end of the iron on the heat until bright red. Press the hot brand against the frame exactly where you prefer your initial to appear; hold in place 10 seconds.

3. Spray glass cleaner directly on a paper towel and wipe the panes clean. To remove any lint, a ball of crumpled newspaper may be more effective against static than the paper towel.

4. Turn the frame upside down. If necessary, remove any hanging hardware from the back of the frame, since you'll want your tray to lie flat on a tabletop. Insert 1 pane of glass into the frame. Sprinkle with 1 layer of petals, scattering to fill frame. Top with the second pane of glass.

5. Use the end of the putty knife to insert glazing points into each side of the frame to hold the glass securely in place. Position each point 2 inches from each corner; the flat side of the point should rest directly on the glass with the tip pointed toward the frame. The notch of the points will fit against the end of the tool; simply push the point into the wood.

MAKES 1 TRAY

peanuts and soda

An afternoon of easy pitch softball has been a
favorite ritual of our family get-togethers. We compete
to hit the longest home run and everyone feels like an all-star.
How better to cheer for the home team than by serving
ballpark flavors of icy root beer with individual sacks of
peanuts and pistachios served up in a vintage soda crate.

INGREDIENTS

1. Fill pouches halfway with mix of nuts, about ¼ cup per bag.
2. Place 1 pouch with nuts in each slot of soda crate.

MAKES 24 SERVINGS

**24 2-inch-wide glassine
pouches with gusset,
available at restaurant
suppliers**

large bag roasted peanuts

large bag pistachios

soda crate

Nutrition Fac
Serv Size 1 bottle (
Total Fat 0g (0% DV
Protein 0g (0% DV)

water bottles

Recycling is a sensible strategy to minimize the waste that ends up in our community landfills. I've found a way to reuse long-necked wine and vinegar bottles: After a good cleaning, they make beautiful carafes. Use vinyl transfers, press-on type (available in craft and stationery stores), or stickers to create your own personal label. For parties, I put a fresh face on bottled water by serving filtered tap water in monogrammed bottles. Used corks make logical and excellent stoppers.

MATERIALS

wine bottles

bottle brush

press-on initials, 1 per bottle

1. Wash used bottles thoroughly with hot, soapy water and a bottle brush. Dry.
2. Rub on 1 press-on letter to the face of each bottle.

kraft paper table runner

Keeping it easy on Labor Day is the only sensible way to set your table. Forget linens, which need to be washed and pressed, and opt instead for kraft paper. This plain brown paper is a versatile addition to your party pantry. It makes a great table overlay, and after dinner you can simply wad it up and toss it into your recycling bin, or use it to kindle a bonfire. I buy rolls of this affordable paper at office suppliers and use it often. You can personalize the paper with quotes, decorations, or guests' names, using crayons or rubber stamps— I like to leave a few coffee mugs filled with crayons on the table so our guests can doodle. Use customized cocktail napkins as coasters. These are extremely affordable when ordered by the hundred, and you'll have them on hand for many occasions. Stationery purveyors are your best source; allow at least 2 weeks to receive them.

MATERIALS

1 roll kraft paper

scissors

1 2-inch-wide or 3-inch-wide smooth stone per guest

1. Unroll and cut the paper to cover the length of your table. If you have a narrow table, the roll of paper should be wide enough. For wider tables, cut the paper in half along the mid-line. Lay the twin runners along each side of the table directly under dinner plates.
2. Set with flatware and glassware. Use stones to anchor a napkin at each place setting.

fire pit

Fire is mesmerizing. Its warm, crackling, explosive energy is impossible to resist. Telling stories, making music, toasting and tasting the night away is one of my favorite ways to wind up a summery day. We began with a small circle of stones for our first pit, but our addiction grew, so we dug deeper and widened the circle to make room for more chairs to gather round and space to cook. In a local quarry, we chose rocks with flat faces, which are easier to stack, and inexpensive pea gravel for ground cover around the base.

MATERIALS

shovel

100 football-sized field-stone rocks with flat faces

15 large, flat flagstones (often used for garden paths)

5-pound bag quick-mix concrete

3 25-pound bags pea gravel

1. Choose a clear, level area to dig a hole 5 feet in diameter and 15 inches deep. Bury 5 of the flattest large field stones in the center of the circle so that the flat tops of the rock make a base. Line the wall of the shallow pit with a ring of rocks.

2. Beginning with the largest rocks, create a wall around the pit, layering the rocks so that the flat sides balance against other rocks. For the best fire management, be sure to stack the rocks so that there are natural vents between them around the circumference. Continue to build to a height of 15 inches. Examine your wall, restack any section that seems wobbly, and cement key rocks together.

3. Bury the additional 10 large, flat flagstones around the pit to create a pleasing random foundation around the wall. Next, spread bags of pea gravel around the pit and stones to fill in any bare areas and to create a radiating pattern. Stomp the pebbles in place with your boots. The stones will be packed down properly after one rainstorm.

campfire potatoes

Cooking outdoors is smoky adventure. The key to a well-cooked meal over coals begins with a good fire. Our pit is large enough to hold a flat grate or grill about 2 feet in diameter, and has short legs (about 5 inches tall). I found mine at a garage sale, but a round barbecue grill rack and bricks for legs that allows air to circulate under the wood work, too. When ready, shovel a good coal base to the side of the fire for cooking. Keep a pair of heat-resistant work gloves by the campfire to use when tending the grill.

MATERIALS

fork

6 large baking potatoes

heavy-duty foil

20 pages of newspaper

metal grill or basket with feet

10 sticks, 2-inch x 2-inch x 10-inch kindling

hatchet

aged logs

torch

shovel

salt and pepper

1 stick butter

1 cup thick Greek-style plain yogurt

½ cup chopped chives

1. Use fork tines to poke a series of holes around the potato before wrapping each snugly with heavy-duty foil. Set aside.
2. Crunch up 15 single pages of newspaper into a loose ball and pack them all under the grill. Ball up the additional paper and place on top of the grill.
3. Make a teepee over the newspaper with a stack of dry kindling. (Collect dry branches from your yard or use a hatchet to cut down a log into 2-inch-wide sticks.) Make a tripod over the kindling with 3 skinny logs (split wood logs if necessary to make easier to burn lengths.) Ignite the newspaper. As the kindling burns, add more kindling or paper until the logs burn; add another log and let the fire burn hot to create a bed of coals. Add more wood as necessary.
4. Push a pile of ashy, glowing coals with the shovel to the side of the fire. Lay foil-wrapped potatoes on the coals, and top with more coals. Stir after 10 minutes; let cook for about 25 minutes or until soft.
5. Garnish with freshly ground salt and pepper, a pat of butter, a dollop of plain yogurt, and freshly chopped chives.

MAKES 6 SERVINGS

cookie sandwiches

S'mores are a campfire favorite. Finding long, green branches and whittling them to a fine point for skewering marshmallows was a job we'd fight for as kids. Only the most prudent were allowed to wield the sharp jackknife. The art of roasting a perfect marshmallow became a competitive sport, and many, many marshmallows were sacrificed in perfecting our techniques. The recipe of molten mallow squished between graham crackers and a chocolate square is yummy in the way that only something sweet, sticky, and sentimental can be. A less sweet but still flavorful alternative requires no heat, can be prepared in moments, and is guaranteed to have guests smacking their lips for more.

INGREDIENTS

64 graham cracker cookies

8 ounces cream cheese

4 ounces raspberry jam

1. Spread ¼ ounce of cream cheese on 1 cookie; top with a thin layer of jam.
2. Top with second cookie.

MAKES 32 SANDWICHES

halloween

Fall is a bewitching time of year. Flocks of honking geese signal the summer farewell as leaves repaint the skyline with a gold and ruby fringe. The season's relentless march toward winter is marked with vivid beauty, and when the harvest moon rises preposterously low on the horizon, I'm tempted to howl with delight. Halloween has always been a night to be cheeky and unveil your alter ego. Invite friends to a moonlight masquerade with a note attached to a simple black mask that you request guests to wear. Set the table with stylized pumpkins and feast by candlelight; serve a frothy brew and retell spooky yarns. This hallowed eve says "Welcome" rather than "Beware."

bittersweet art

To create an instant dramatic décor in any plain room, I often hang prestretched canvas that I paint in complementary colors. For Halloween I crafted a three-dimensional "painting" by hanging a wreath of bittersweet branches to the painted canvas.

MATERIALS

3-inch-wide paintbrush or small roller

½ quart of orange acrylic or matte latex paint

1 3-foot x 3-foot prestretched, primed canvas with a one-inch frame, available at art supply stores

12 feet of bittersweet branches, available at farmers markets, floral crafts, and backyards

2 12-inch lengths of 24-gauge floral wire

30 inches 26-gauge paper-covered wire, available in florist's supply shops

wire clippers

2 wine corks

1. Using a brush or roller, evenly cover an already-primed canvas with a coat of orange paint. Once it's dry, repeat if you'd like a more saturated color. (Acrylic and latex paints are simple to apply, quick to dry, and easy to clean off with water.)

2. Select bittersweet branches with the most berries and bend into a rough 2-foot-wide circle. Spiral the branches to make a simple wreath shape. Rest on flat surface.

3. Mark 3 equidistant points around the circumference of the wreath shape. At each point, twist 3-inch lengths of wired twine to connect adjacent branches and to maintain the circular shape. The tendrils of the bittersweet will help, as they naturally entwine. Anchor vines together at 3 additional points around the circumference. (It's necessary to maintain a round shape.) Trim excess wire with clippers.

4. The wreath will be asymmetrical because of the rambling nature of the vine. Determine the top point. With a twist, attach one length of florist's wire to a branch near the top of the underside of the wreath. Center the wreath over the canvas, find the position you like best, then poke the wire attached to the underside of the wreath through the canvas to create an attachment point. Wrap the wire around the center of one cork and poke the wire end back through the canvas, pull taut, and attach to the wreath with a twist to secure the wreath to the canvas. Repeat the process to anchor the bottom half of the wreath.

MAKES 1 WREATH

mini-graveyard

I've always had a fascination with graveyards. I go out of my way to visit old, crumbly ones that seem forgotten but are clearly made hallow by the departed. Formal, densely packed avenues of Victorian temples, churchyard lawns paved with stone, meadows of marble—I've taken pictures of them all. Like other Latinos who honor their departed loved ones with a graveside picnic on the Day of the Dead (the day after Halloween), I even find spooky cemeteries a sanctuary. One day, stumbling through a favorite botanical emporium, I found a magnificent fan of coral. I knew that in the right setting it might double as a haunted tree centerpiece and then live on in my bathroom as a beautiful aquatic sculpture.

MATERIALS

1. Attach felt feet at each corner of the back of the frame. Flip over.
2. Fill the frame with bun moss, tucking the mounds together to create little hills. Aim to create a tiny valley in the center for the tree.
3. Plant the coral at the spot in the moss that looks the best.
4. Use permanent marker or pen and ink to inscribe little rocks with *RIP*. Place randomly in moss.

1 weather-beaten frame with glass or mirror intact

4 1-inch self-adhesive felt rounds, sold packaged to protect tabletops

enough moss to fill in the frame

1 fan of dry coral with root stump

3 small stones with flat surfaces

fine-point white permanent ink pen

harlequin vase

Burnt orange—the color of pumpkins, vivacious dahlias, vivid sunsets, and a well-stoked fire—is also the color of some masking tapes. (I'm always surprised at what I find in my local hardware store, and orange tape was a timely discovery.) The tape adds a bold stroke of color to the evening, a tongue-in-cheek moment for a vase to masquerade as a harlequin.

MATERIALS

1 vase

1 roll 1-inch-wide orange masking tape

scissors

1. Clean and dry vase.

2. Starting at the underside of the vase, tape a vertical stripe of masking tape along the length of the vase. Cut in a clean, straight line just over the lip of the top of the vase.

3. Repeat to encircle the vase with vertical strips of tape.

4. Rub the tape in place with your thumb to eliminate any air bubbles.

5. Fill with water and flowers.

golden pumpkins

It's a rare fruit that can be enjoyed only in the fall, so I look forward to the pumpkin season. I love the sturdy, bold squash, but, once cut, even the most benign jack o'lanterns become frightening when bacteria has time to play at room temperature. Since I want them to last for a month or so, my solution is not to cut but to gild them. I cluster small golden pumpkins and mason jars filled with floating candles for a boo-tiful centerpiece.

MATERIALS

1. In a well-ventilated area, spray the tops of pumpkins with adhesive spray. Spritz (don't saturate) to achieve an irregular pattern over the top half of the pumpkin surface.
2. Once the surface is tacky, rub a sheet of gold leaf tissue over the pumpkin surface. Smudge the tissue in place with your fingers. Use a second sheet if necessary to burnish the upper portion of the pumpkin.
3. Continue rubbing until all the sticky surface area is gilded and loose flecks of gold leaf are smoothed away. Decorated pumpkins may last a month or more.

adhesive spray

assorted mini-pumpkins, preferably with stems

2 sheets of gold-leaf tissue per 4-inch pumpkin, available at art supply stores

spooky cider

A witchy brew of hearty cider is an easy concoction if you have one secret ingredient: dry ice. This is simply frozen carbon dioxide, readily available from any ice house. When exposed to air, dry ice dissolves into a frothy mist. A small amount goes a long way, but it must be handled carefully: Dry ice is so cold, it can "burn" if you touch it without protection. The ice house typically wraps it for sale in newspaper, which is a natural insulator. Small amounts last only a few hours, so purchase it late in the afternoon of your party. When you're ready to serve, drop a small cube of dry ice into each mug to turn it into a mini-cauldron.

MATERIALS

1 gallon of your favorite cider

5 pounds of dry ice (often the minimum sold)

ice pick

tongs

ice bucket

rubber gloves

1 mug per guest

drinking straws

1. Use a large pitcher, punch bowl, or even a large stewpot to hold the cider; flavor it, if you like, with cinnamon sticks and cloves. Cider can be serve warm or at room temperature.

2. Keeping the brick of dry ice in a cooler lined with newspaper, use an ice pick to crack it into ice cube–sized pieces. Place fragments in an ice bucket to serve. (Use rubber gloves or tongs when handling.) Wrap the remainder with newspaper and store in the cooler.

3. Pour a cup of cider into each mug.

4. Use tongs to place a cube into each mug.

5. Serve immediately with a straw to protect lips from the dissolving cube of ice.

MAKES 1 GALLON

candy bar

Trick or treat? When I was a child, knocking on each door in my neighborhood was hard work, but the rewards easily lasted a month or more. Everyone has a sweet tooth at Halloween, so no matter what else you serve, candy must be on the menu. Fill your favorite vessels with your childhood favorites or simply offer black and orange sweets only. Glass carafes and pitchers make it easy to pour candies, or use a scoop for wide-mouth jars.

MATERIALS

1. Fill each container with one type of candy.
2. Fold napkin in half and knot around the belly of the measuring bowl; use a scoop to serve the candies.

   MAKES 12 SERVINGS

ice bucket

4 pounds orange slices

measuring bowl

4 pounds licorice wheels

carafe

2 pounds each orange and black chocolate lentils

1 orange gingham napkin

scoop

orange
night light

Giant glass globes are hardworking vessels. I use these bubbles for many jobs, from floating candles to serving punch to nesting mini-ecosystems. The orb, like a picture window, allows a perfect view of its contents, which seem to float in space. These vases, widely known as bubble bowls, are affordable and versatile. Interestingly, because of their spherical shape, the bowls are sturdy even though they're glass. The flat bottom makes them easy to stack for storage.

MATERIALS

5 feet of bittersweet branch fragments

16-inch bubble bowl

12-inch-tall glass cylinder or apothecary jar that can fit inside the mouth of the bubble bowl

2 cups sand, loose gravel, or cat litter

1 6-inch pillar candle to fit inside the 12-inch cylinder

long-necked butane torch

1. Insert branches of bittersweet into the bubble bowl. Aim to make branches spiral to allow room to insert the narrow glass cylinder into the bowl.
2. Fill bottom of glass cylinder with sand or cat litter. Insert candle, nesting it securely in the sand.
3. Insert cylinder with candle into bubble bowl. The sand's weight will keep the cylinder and candle securely in place. When ready, use a long-necked butane torch to light the candle.

thanksgiving

Of all the holidays, I find Thanksgiving the most endearing—
and the most challenging. The annual debate begins early about
where to meet for Thanksgiving. Once we had our own home, we
naturally wanted a turn to host the big event, blending elements
from our family rituals to create our own, but preparing an entire
feast for the first time is daunting. A potluck meal is a wonderful
solution for new nesters—it's an easier way for everyone to
participate in the feast, much as they did at the Pilgrims' celebrated
meal. The key task is to organize the contributions well in advance
so that everyone brings a favorite dish and there's no overlap. Take
the time to choose wines for each course to enhance the experience
and to give everyone another reason to give thanks.

grapes and rye centerpiece

A stone urn that I found at a flower center has a noble, classical shape. Although it's meant for a garden, I've found it a versatile vessel for centerpieces. For a feast celebrating the fall harvest, combine dry shafts of rye or wheat with bunches of fresh grapes for an edible arrangement, or consider using fabulous fakes, available at craft centers, to create a lasting centerpiece to enjoy all season long. Position a pair on a mantel or just one on an accent table.

MATERIALS

6- to 8-inch-wide plastic dish

urn with an 8-inch mouth

5 bunches of grapes, mixed green and red

clippers

15 stems of rye or wheat, available at craft stores and dried-flower specialists

1. Insert the plastic dish into the top of the urn to create a shallow platform to hold the grapes. You can also fill the bottom of the urn with plastic bags (use recycled supermarket bags), making them compact so that there is a firm foundation inside the vase.

2. If using fresh grapes, make the centerpiece no more than one day before the holiday. Wash grapes and trim the stems of any bruised, discarded fruits. Fill the top of the urn with grapes.

3. Clip stems of rye or wheat to fit in the shallow dish. Group 3 to 4 stems together; tuck them randomly between sections of the grapes.

magnolia leaves

I miss the majestic southern magnolia tree that stood in my parents' front yard. It greeted us with a canopy of enormous, waxy leaves. Lush, fragrant flowers bloomed each spring and the leaves stayed green all year. Make a rustic welcome to sit on your front stoop with a bowl full of leafy branches—substitute pine or rhododendron if more readily available—and nestle them into a willow trellis (garden centers stock them for protecting rose plants).

1. Working on an ironing surface, thread ribbon through D-ring buckle to create a 10-inch end. Place one layer of fusing tape along the 10-inch section of ribbon on the other side of the buckle, and sandwich the fusing tape by folding the extending 10-inch end of ribbon on the other end of the buckle over the tape. Use a hot iron to fuse the sections together, anchoring the buckle at one end of the ribbon. Trim other end with sharp scissors. Set aside.
2. Fill bowl with sand and arrange clipped branches in the sand. Cut branches again, if necessary, to create a densely packed bowl of leaves.
3. Buckle the ribbon belt loosely around the 24-inch mark of the willow cylinder. Loosen until the top of the trellis can open wide enough for the bowl to rest at the top of the trellis. Tighten the ribbon belt to secure.

MATERIALS

1 yard of 1-inch-wide brown grosgrain ribbon

1 set D-ring buckle, available at sewing centers

10 inches of fusing tape

iron

scissors

15-inch-wide ceramic bowl

1 gallon sand

20 leafy branches of magnolia, clipped 15 inches long

36-inch cylinder willow trellis

cabernet

wineglass labels

The way to have a proper wine tasting is with a crowd.
Thanksgiving is a perfect opportunity to sample some of the superb
and affordable wines on the market. Although I have some favorites,
I rely on experts to guide my choices. When you find a wine store
that you like—it should be convenient, stock affordable wines from
around the world, and deliver—get to know the buyer or owner.
Ask for suggestions on a regular basis to establish your preferences.
We have a mixed case of favorites delivered every month. With
good advice you'll be sure to have a collection of just the right wines
for special occasions. For Thanksgiving, consider selecting wines
that represent the different hometown regions of your guests.

MATERIALS

1 yard kraft paper

3-inch hole punch

scissors

¼-inch hole punch

marker

1. Cut 3-inch holes from sheet of kraft paper.
2. Use scissors to cut the radius (a straight line from the center of the circle to the circumference).
3. Use the ¼-inch punch to cut a center hole in the disc to accommodate the stem of the wineglass. If necessary, make a second punch to expand the hole to fit the wine stem.
4. Use a marker to note the type of wine, its place of origin, and its vintage.

cork flags

A feast with wine is not complete without a cheese course, served early, as hors d'oeuvres, or later, for dessert. When serving a selection of cheeses, mix the types and their sources of milk for a more interesting tasting: a hard-rind cheese like Parmesan, pungent blues, fresh goat cheeses, creamy sheep's milk cheeses, and my favorite, a super-mature cheddar. Serve with crusty bread and a mix of olives (don't forget a small discard bowl for pits) on breadboards. Identify cheeses with champagne cork flags.

1. Cut business card–sized flags from sheet of card stock.
2. Stamp each card with an acorn-stamped impression.
3. Use marker to identify each cheese served.
4. Anchor flag to champagne cork or directly into a hard cheese with the stickpin.

MATERIALS

1 sheet 8-inch x 11-inch taupe card stock

paper cutter or scissors

rubber stamp

green ink pad

magenta marker

paper clip stick pins, available at office supply stores

champagne corks

HUMBOLDT FOG
CHEVRE

PARMIGIANO
REGGIANO

BAYLEY HAZEN
RAW MILK BLUE

homespun cozy

Slippers for stemware? Fancy great-grandmothers protected wood tables with monogrammed cloth sleeves for their stemware. The comforting linens, known as cozies, also dressed the table with a certain charm. To protect our rustic pine table from sweaty ice-water goblets, I wrap the base with a swatch of homespun twine.

MATERIALS

1 yard burlap

scissors

12 goblets

1 yard kitchen twine

1. Cut 5-inch squares from the yard of fabric.
2. Center goblet on fabric square, wrap base, and tie in place with twine.
   MAKES 12 COZIES

wire napkin ring

It's a **marvelous example** of a simple, beautiful solution. The braided wire cage that secures champagne corks is so clever, yet elegant, it's remained virtually unchanged since the first twist. Once removed from the bubbly bottle, the structure of the cage easily becomes a napkin ring, or use wire clippers to make petite chairs ideal to hold place cards. Menus are 4-inch by 7-inch sheets of kraft paper. I use a combination of rubber stamps and markers to list the courses.

MATERIALS

champagne cage

wire clippers

24-inch linen napkin

iron

1. Untwist collar. Clip the center of the loop and pull the collar through the four brackets. Open cage to a flat *X*.
2. Press napkin, fold in half, press down fold. Fold in half again and press down fold.
3. Roll napkin into a cylinder. Center cage around the middle of the napkin. Mold the wire around the napkin to secure in place.

MAKES 1 NAPKIN WRAP

WIRE CHAIR

Wrapping a napkin with the cage is easy, but twisting the wire to create a little chair takes some practice. Snip and remove the collar. Shape the four points of the cage into a stool shape, then use the collar to twist each end around adjacent legs, rounding out the center to create a chair back.

butternut squash soup

The thermal glass used for canning is a handsome, homey way to serve soup. The pint-sized jars make perfect individual servings. They're also easy to stack and look fabulous on a wood platter for a holiday buffet or to serve to seated guests. Serve with crusty rolls.

INGREDIENTS

2 tablespoons extra-virgin olive oil

1 celery stalk, chopped

1 medium onion, chopped

1 medium carrot, chopped

1 medium butternut squash

chef's knife

½ pound potatoes for boiling, peeled and cubed

2 teaspoons coarse sea salt

4 cups boiling water

8 1 cup mason jar with lid

red pepper flakes

1. Heat oil in a heavy 3-quart saucepan over low heat. Add celery, onion, and carrot. Stir once a minute, until tender, about 10 minutes.

2. Peel squash with a chef's knife. The skin is thick—I find it easiest to slice off the top and bottom of the squash first, so it sits solidly on the cutting board. Then continue to peel the sides of the squash. Remove and discard pith and seeds.

3. Add squash, potatoes, and salt to cooking vegetables. Stir together and add boiling water. Lower to simmer, and cook about 20 minutes, until all vegetables are tender to the fork.

4. Cool and purée soup in small batches in a food processor (for small quantities I prefer to use a counter-friendly mini-chopper). If necessary, add water or vegetable stock to thin.

5. Pour ½ cup servings into each mason jar, garnish with a sprinkle of red pepper flakes.

MAKES 8 SERVINGS

oak leaf votive

Votives are the easiest way to decorate without breaking the bank. These glass cylinders are versatile, can be dressed in many ways, and are infinitely reusable. Inspired by the season, I travel no farther than our backyard to make a forest of fall votives to scatter everywhere.

MATERIALS

1. Wrap the oak leaf around the glass.
2. Wrap the wired grapevine around the center vein of the leaf; twist to cinch securely in place. Tuck any leaf ends taller than the votive back under the grapevine.

MAKES 1 VOTIVE WRAP

1 pliable, freshly fallen oak leaf

6 inches wired grapevine, available in craft shops

2-inch glass votive

winter solstice

Cozy blankets, evergreen trees, candlelight, mugs of hot chocolate—these are just a few of my favorite things about winter. But winter is a season of extremes. I don't love being so cold that I can feel every little hair standing at attention, and I don't love digging out from a big snow (again) or desalting my favorite shoes (again), but I do love the crackle of the fireplace, the whisper of falling snow, and the comfort of my downy bed and warm arms of my mate. Winter, like every time of year, has its charms. To toast the season I collect a harvest from our backyard. Weathered woods, nuts and pinecones, fragrant branches and curling vines—the remains of the year are elegant artifacts that need little if any adornment.

backyard
ornaments

There's no place like home, the birds in my backyard remind me every winter. Yes, there are worlds to travel—every day, geese and osprey bank just over our roof on their long trip south. Yet it's the birds that prefer to stay close to the nest that warm my heart and bring life to the quiet yard as they look for ready treats and the gratification that can be found at home. To coax the birds I decorate the yard with grapevine balls with stems of millet and chunks of suet (available at pet supply stores), along with silver bells in the trees. I've found well-priced grapevine ornaments at floral suppliers and craft shops—they also look great stacked in a bowl for a centerpiece. You can make your own with cuttings.

MATERIALS

10 yards grapevine, willow, or other long, pliable vine

1 inflatable exercise ball (available in toy stores)

clippers

10-inch length wired twine

1. Accumulate clippings (they can be of assorted lengths). If using woody vines, soak them first in a tub of hot water for an hour.
2. Inflate an exercise ball to 8 inches in diameter.
3. Wrap vine around the ball and knot in place with a twist of twine. Continue to wrap the vine around the ball in a twisting, crisscross style. Use small twists of twine to stabilize vine wherever needed.
4. When finished, deflate ball (reusable to make additional orbs), remove from center of vines. Use wired twine to suspend the vine ornament from a tree branch.

MAKES 1 8-INCH BALL

ribbon wreath

Wreaths are wonderful decorative elements.
With the simplest of materials it's easy to make the most luxurious
punctuation to hang anywhere in your home. For the holidays I love
to hang multiple wreaths: one by the front door, another over the
wood-burning stove, another above the love seat, one more in the
courtyard. I play with all sorts of materials: grapevine balls, ornaments,
clusters of fake grapes (they look so real), bittersweet berries,
evergreens, and herbs. Unless you plan to hang a pair of wreaths
together in one room or on opposite sides of your front door, they
don't have to match each other. To hang a wreath, position it as
you would a painting, just above eye level; use a picture hook that
holds the appropriate weight to secure the wreath to the wall.

1. Cut the ribbon into 15-inch lengths, keeping colors separate.
2. Tie the first ribbon securely around the cross-section of the ring into
   a fluffy bow.
3. Repeat with remaining ribbons, alternating colors in the same order.
   When done, be sure all bows face the front face of the wreath. The
   bows should be densely packed. Tighten bows and fluff in place.
4. Use the shears to cut a swallow-tail end to each ribbon. To cut, fold
   the end of the ribbon in half at the center point. Cut a diagonal line
   from the 2-inch point to the outer corner. Use clean, sharp scissors
   for a smooth, straight cut.

MAKES 1 WREATH

MATERIALS

90 feet 4-inch-wide satin
ribbon, 30 feet each in gold,
copper, and bronze

sharp shears

18-inch wire wreath frame,
available at floral suppliers
and craft shops

starfish tree

A hike through the forest, a walk on the beach, or a stroll to my favorite dried-flower shop turn up all sorts of botanical objects of beauty. Natural elements have a sculptural appeal that deserve to be admired. Often I simply present them scattered throughout my home in bowls and trays, but sometimes a branchy root begs to be turned upside down, becoming a wintry tree. Adding shell ornaments to my bare shrub is a folly that makes me smile. The natural wood looks positively stately in a stone urn filled with smooth white stones.

MATERIALS

1-pound bag quick-mix or ready-mix craft plaster, available in craft shops

root or rootlike branch, ideally with a 20-inch canopy

10-inch stone or plaster urn

2-cup empty plastic carton

4 cups smooth white stones

20 starfish

20 8-inch lengths thin metal wire

clippers

1. Mix ½ bag of quick-mix plaster, according to package directions, or use ready-mix plaster to fill the plastic carton.
2. Insert long-stem end of the branch into the plaster. If using more than one branch, space carefully to create a tree shape. Support branches in place while plaster hardens.
3. Place plaster carton in urn. Place stones under and around the carton to stabilize. Be sure tree looks level. Add additional stones on top to conceal plaster.
4. Twist wire around center of each starfish to attach to the branches in a random, appealing way.

birch tree

I love that a simple log sliced into 2-inch discs can be restacked to create a whimsical tree for a charming holiday centerpiece. Bits of moss imitate evergreen thatch, and a tiny birdhouse, sold as a paint-it-yourself ornament in a craft store, makes a charming topper.

MATERIALS

1. Use a chain saw to cut logs into 2-inch slices. (Precut wood discs are available seasonally at nurseries and floral supply shops.)
2. Stack the wood slices into a tapered tower to resemble a tree with the 10-inch ring as the base. Stagger the wood slices so that they do not line up evenly. Mark a point through the cross-section of each disc where a dowel, when inserted, will be able to skewer each disc in a straight line yet maintain the staggered pattern.
3. At these markings, use the drill to cut a ¼-inch hole through the entire centers of all but one of the 4-inch-wide and all of the 6-inch-wide discs. When complete, the holes should line up while the discs maintain the askew pattern.
4. Drill a hole only halfway through the center of the 10-inch disc and the remaining 4-inch disc. Restack the discs and insert the dowel through the holes; insert the bottom end of dowel into the 10-inch disc. Pull the discs apart so that they have a ½-inch gap between each layer. Clip the emerging length of dowel to two inches.
5. Before attaching the top disc, drill a hole ⅛-inch deep in the center of the disc with a ¹⁄₁₆-inch bit. Drill a hole in the center of the bottom of the birdhouse. Clip the bamboo skewer into a 3-inch stick; twist each end into the ¹⁄₁₆-inch-holes to connect birdhouse to top of the tree.
6. Place tree construction on the tray. Tuck sections of moss between each layer, reserving enough moss to cover the tray and most of the base.

MATERIALS

1 6-inch-wide birch log

1 4-inch-wide birch log

1 10-inch-wide birch log

chain saw

drill with ¼-inch bit, ¹⁄₁₆-inch bit

2-foot-long ¼-inch dowel

bamboo skewer

flower clippers

2 square feet moss

12-inch round tray

miniature wood birdhouse, available at craft stores, whitewashed with 50-50 mix of white paint and water

fancy flutes

We enjoy champagne—or any of its wonderful variations—
all year. Spending Friday evenings together at home is one of our
favorite reasons to drink it. For the winter holidays, it seems fitting to
dress up our everyday flutes with some finery. I find thin satin ribbons
to be the most versatile. The result is exuberant and tailored at the
same time. Braid silver and gold for a luxurious holiday note, and knot
securely at the stem. Trim with sharp scissors to make a fresh fringe.
Even though this detail takes no more than two minutes to execute,
you'll gain even more time-saving thrills knowing that the ribbons
will run through the dishwasher and look fresh for additional holiday
toasts. The coaster is a holiday ornament I found in the paint-it-
yourself section of my favorite craft store; I sprayed it gold.

MATERIALS

2 champagne flutes

2 ³⁄₈-inch-wide silver ribbon,
10-inches in length

2 ³⁄₈-inch-wide gold ribbon,
10-inches in length

scissors

1. Using 1 of each color per flute, hold 2 ribbons together at their center
   point. Start at the top of the stem, wrap the ribbons around the neck
   of the flute. Pull ribbons securely with each wrap to be sure the
   ribbons lie flat and crisscross. Knot together at the base into a loopy,
   rabbit-ear bow. Pull taut.

2. Use sharp scissors and cut through the center of each bow or ear.
   Trim ribbon ends at an angle to make a 1-inch fringe.

winter window box

When snow is on the ground, the view from my bedroom window is hard to resist on a moonlit night. The downy evergreens in our cozy yard surround a brilliant meadow of powder—it's a snapshot from a dream. Inspired, I made wintry window boxes with feathered cones for trees and soap flakes for snow. This winterscape makes a perfect holiday centerpiece.

MATERIALS

1 plain wooden window box

2-inch x 4-inch wood, cut to fit snugly inside the length of your box

4 2-inch finishing nails

hammer

wood filler

drill with 1/16-inch bit

1 can white spray paint

20 sheets white tissue paper

4 sheets thin 8-inch x 11-inch cardboard

stapler

utility scissors

tube white craft glue

bag of white craft feathers

4 bamboo skewers

3 cups laundry-soap flakes

1. Insert 2-inch x 4-inch wood into the window box so that the 2-inch side rests along the center of the base of the box. Use 2 finishing nails to anchor it to the end of the box. Cover nail with a dab of wood filler.

2. Spray entire box with white paint; apply second coat. Drill 4 equidistant 1/16-inch holes along the center beam. Use tissue paper to fill gaps on each side of the beam.

3. Roll each cardboard sheet to create a simple cone with a 3-inch base. Staple flaps to hold the shape. Trim remnant board so the cone is level. Spray white.

4. Starting at the bottom of the cone, use a dab of craft glue to attach a row of white feathers about 2 inches from the base. Determine the right starting point by the length of your feathers. Repeat to cover the cones with feathers.

5. Squirt a dab of wood filler into the top of the cone; let set. When it's dry, insert the pointed end of the skewer inside into the cone's center and the other end into one of the 4 holes.

6. Scatter laundry-soap flakes about the base of the trees to cover the tissue paper.

monogram napkins

Especially in candlelight, winter parties seem best dressed in finer threads. I pull out my fanciest china and crystal, which mix well with everyday white classics when I need to set a table for a crowd. I top a basic white cotton tablecloth with two yards of lace that I picked up on sale at a fabric discounter. I cut around the openwork motifs instead of cutting a straight line, and in short order I had an elegant topper without adding a stitch. In the notions area of the craft store I found block letters with heat-sensitive adhesive backing that I pressed onto the corners of each of our white linen napkins for instant monograms.

MATERIALS

iron, without water

1 dozen white linen napkins

1 dozen 2-inch block letters with adhesive backing

white cotton pressing cloth or old T-shirt

1. Heat dry iron to cotton setting. Press the napkin into a folded square.

2. At one corner, place one letter diagonally 1 inch from the point. Cover with the pressing cloth, and apply the iron for 10 to 15 seconds at a time to heat and press the letter in place. The adhesive should take hold within 1 minute.

3. Fold the napkin into a shape that shows off the monogram.

hot chocolate

A roaring fire, a table set to sparkle, candlelight everywhere, seasonal classics recorded to a jazzy beat that fills the air with a holiday hum, and the happy chatter of loved guests— that's my idea of a fine celebration. Hearty, flavorful courses are the cornerstones of every end-of-the-year feast; freely blending family favorites with new tastes. Whether you opt to have a simple-to-execute dinner of quick-to-roast loin of pork with a savory compote of onions and apples, or a cultural favorite like lasagna, tamales, or roast duckling, round out the evening with a mug of comfort.

INGREDIENTS

1. Coarsely chop chocolate with a chef's knife. Melt chocolate in a double boiler, stirring chocolate continuously until melted. Gradually add sugar to chocolate, whisk until well blended.
2. In a nonreactive pan, heat milk until hot; do not boil. Slowly add milk to chocolate mix; whisk until well blended. While stirring, bring chocolate mix to simmer.
3. Whisk cornstarch mix into hot chocolate; simmer. Pour into mugs wrapped with satin ribbon. Serve with a dollop of whipped cream, cinnamon, and a waffle cookie.

MAKES 4 SERVINGS

3½ ounces semisweet chocolate

chef's knife

saucepan of simmering water

3 tablespoons sugar

whisk

nonreactive saucepan (stainless, glass or ceramic)

1 quart whole milk

½ teaspoon cornstarch, mixed well with 2 tablespoons cold water

1 cup whipped cream (see page 91)

4 waffle cookies

shaker ground cinnamon

4 8-inch lengths of gold satin ribbon

party registry

Take the time to register for items that will equip your pantry and home with versatile goods that will make parties even easier to produce. I suggest stocking up on a few extra essentials—like a dozen white dinner plates and linen napkins for large parties. Select a base pattern that's easy to mix with a variety of decorative accents to suit a variety of occasions. Choosing classic elements always makes sense, making it simple to embellish your collection anytime. Here is a checklist of helpful items.

- ☐ white dinner plates
- ☐ linen napkins
- ☐ colorful accent plates for salad, dessert, and lunch
- ☐ colorful cups and saucers
- ☐ mugs for coffee or soups
- ☐ tall soup/cereal bowls; use also for condiments and snacks
- ☐ low soup bowls for pasta
- ☐ stainless flatware
- ☐ goblets
- ☐ red and white wine glasses
- ☐ champagne flutes
- ☐ double old-fashioned glasses; use also for iced tea and mixing
- ☐ pitcher
- ☐ carafe
- ☐ ice bucket
- ☐ serving platters and bowls

- ☐ tray
- ☐ gravy boat, use also for side dishes
- ☐ serving forks, spoons, ladle
- ☐ steak knives
- ☐ coffee maker or press
- ☐ grinder
- ☐ mixing bowls
- ☐ sturdy blender
- ☐ cork screw
- ☐ shaker, stirrer
- ☐ bottle opener
- ☐ chopping board
- ☐ whisk
- ☐ cheese grater
- ☐ micro plane
- ☐ measuring cups and spoons
- ☐ paring, serrated, and chef's knives

- ☐ sharpening steel
- ☐ kitchen shears, scissors
- ☐ dish towels
- ☐ stainless skillet
- ☐ 2-quart, 3-quart saucepans
- ☐ 6-quart stockpot
- ☐ wok
- ☐ griddle
- ☐ pot lids
- ☐ roasting pan
- ☐ cast-iron skillet
- ☐ wood spoons
- ☐ candles
- ☐ hurricanes and torches
- ☐ sound system
- ☐ throw pillows
- ☐ BBQ grill and tools
- ☐ vases

resources

Use this list of contacts to feather your nest and produce the projects featured in this book. For additional celebration ideas please see my other books, *The Perfect Wedding Details, The Perfect Wedding Reception* and *The Perfect Wedding* or visit my website, MariaMcBride.com.

ARTS & CRAFTS

All Season Trading Company
allseason.com
800-700-5233
wide variety of beads

Architectural Products
www.archpro.com
800-789-5322
architectural components

Art Store
artstore.com
800-828-4548
art supplies

Beacon Fabric
beaconfabric.com
800-713-8157
sewing supplies, fabrics

Brand-first
brand-first.com
888-583-5353
branding irons

Custom Embossers
customembossers.com
800-606-9655
embossers and wax seals

Fiskars
fiskars.com
tips for paper-cutting tools

Framing Supplies
framingsupplies.com
800-334-9060
frames, tools

Glu Stix
glu-stix.com
877-770-5500
glue guns, supplies

The Gold Leaf Company
goldleafcompany.com
718-815-8802
metal leaf materials, info

Hobby Lobby
hobbylobby.com
crafting supplies

Impact Images
clearbags.com
800-233-2630
transparent packaging

**Jo-Ann Fabric and
Craft Stores**
joann.com
330-656-2600
craft supplies

Kate's Paperie
katespaperie.com
800-809-9880
stationery supplies

Merchants Overseas
merchantsoverseas.com
800-714-7714
Swarovski crystal distributor

Metalliferous
metalliferous.com
888-944-0909
metal wires, tools

Lee Carter Company
leecartercompany.com
415-824-2004
Mexican, Haitian accessories

Mango Trading
casaycocina.com
415-585-4459
Guatemalan linens

Mex Grocer
mexgrocer.com
877-463-9476
Hispanic foods

Pearl River
pearlriver.com
800-878-2446
Joss paper

Send Leis
Sendleis.com
609-720-0300
fresh leis, express delivery

FLORAL ACCESSORIES

Afloral.com
888-299-4100
floral tools, supplies

Allstate Floral & Craft
allstatefloral.com
562-926-2302
faux grapes

Dry Nature
drynature.com
212-695-8911
preserved botanicals, fan coral

Farms to Go
farmstogo.com
800-383-4959
cut flowers by mail

Garden Valley Ranch
gardenvalley.com
707-795-0919
garden roses by mail

Gardenocity
seedlover.com
866-215-2230
Jiffy peat pots

Pany's
panysilkflower.com
212-645-9526
silk flowers

Pro Flowers
proflowers.com
800-580-2913
plants, flowers by mail

U.S. Shell
usshell.com
800-367-8508
shells

GARDEN ACCESSORIES

American Country Home Store
bistropatio.com
800-765-1688
classic bistro chairs

Big Sky Tents
bigskytent.com
617-201-3522
Raj tents, umbrellas

Confetti Bay
confettibay.com
508-824-3501
raffia umbrella

Kelly Scott Designs
kellyscottdesigns.com
215-242-0817
canopies for sale, rent

Outdoor Décor
outdoordecor.com
800-422-1525
torches, arbors and more

Smith and Hawken
smithandhawken.com
800-940-1170
furniture and accessories

W. T. Kirkman
lanternnet.com
877-985-5267
oil lanterns, supplies

HARDWARE

Home Depot
homedepot.com
800-435-4654
appliances, tools

Lowe's Home Improvement
lowes.com
800-445-6937
appliances, tools

A Best Kitchen
abestkitchen.com
888-388-9641
kitchen goods

Anchor Hocking
anchorhocking.com
800-562-7511
kitchen glassware

Bella's Cucina
bellascucina.com
310-306-4734
branding irons for meats

Bodum
bodum.com
800-23-BODUM
brewing supplies

Bowery Restaurant Supply
bowerykitchens.com
212-376-4982
kitchen supplies

Copco
copco.com
800-794-5866
kitchen ware

KitchenAid
kitchenaid.com
800-334-6889
appliances, cookware

Lodge
lodgemfg.com
423-837-7181
cast-iron cookware

Restaurant Source
restaurantsource.com
800-460-8402
kitchen supplies

Specialty Bottle
specialtybottle.com
206-340-0459
glass, tin, plastic bottles

Target
target.com
800-440-0680
kitchen, home goods

Williams-Sonoma
877-812-6235
williams-sonoma.com
cookware, accessories

Battery Operated Candles
batteryoperatedcandles.net
800-879-0537
tea lights

Candles 4 Less
candles4less.com
877-766-5328
candles by the case

Candles Just on Line
candlesjustonline.com
800-375-8023
floating candles:

Crafted Candles
craftedcandles.com
800-635-0274
traditional tapers

Creative Candles
creativecandles.com
800-237-9711
47 color choices

Apec
apec-usa.com
800-221-9403
glassine envelopes

Departure Design
departuredesign.com
631-560-4886
party rentals by mail

DHP Papermill & Press
dhproductions.net
888-454-8151
letterpress confetti

For Your Party
foryourparty.com
866-383-8957
custom printed goods

Home Brew It
homebrewit.com
574-295-9975
empty wine bottles

Jamali Garden Supplies
Jamaligarden.com
212-996-5534
party, floral accessories

Label Lab
Labellab.com
800-952-1457
custom labels

Midori
midoriribbon.com
800-659-3049
imprintable ribbons

Okamoto Studio
okamotostudionyc.com
212-842-0630
ice sculptures

Precidio
Precidio.com
800-387-2304
acrylic stemware

Staples
staples.com
800-378-2753
stationery

Royer Corporation
royercorp.com
800-457-8997
picks, stirrers

PROVISIONS

Boylan Bottling Company
boylanbottling.com
800-289-7978
vintage soda pop

Caviar 4 You
caviar4you.com
201-988-9812
imported and American

The Chef's Garden
chefs-garden.com
800-289-4644
sustainable micro greens

The CMC Company
thecmccompany.com
800-262-2780
hard-to-find foods

Costco
costco.com
800-955-2292
warehouse retailer

Dean & Deluca
deandeluca.com
800-221-7714
foods, kitchen supplies

Easy Leaf Products
easyleafproducts.com
323-769-4827
edible metal leaf

Edible Gold
ediblegold.com
415-407-5097
edible gold leaf

Fancy Flours
fancyflours.com
406-522-8887
sweets, supplies

Kaluystans
kalustyans.com
800-352-3451
international spices

The Little Pearl
littlepearl.com
888-61-Blini
caviar, info

Lobster Gram
livelob.com
800-548-3562
live lobsters by mail

Mitsuwa
mitsuwa.com
asian foods

Mountain Lake Fisheries
whitefishcaviar.com
888-809-0826
whitefish caviar by mail

My Jones
myjones.com
800-656-6050
sodas, custom labels

Sterling Caviar
sterlingcaviar.com
800-525-0333
farmed caviar by mail

Sunburst Trout Company
sunbursttrout.com
800-673-3051
trout caviar by mail

Vermont Country Store
vermontcountrystore.com
802-362-8460
traditional favorites

Whole Foods
wholefoodsmarket.com
organic foods

TABLEWARE

Abigails
abigails.net
800-678-8485
glassware, tableware

Ann Gish
anngish.com
212-969-9200
table and bed linens

Arte Italica
arteitalica.com
212-213-4773
porcelain, pewter dinnerware

Bed, Bath and Beyond
bedbathandbeyond.com
800-462-3966
housewares

Bloomingdale's
bloomingdales.com
800-472-0788

Crate & Barrel
crateandbarrel.com
800-967-6696
housewares

Dansk
dansk.com
800-326-7528
contemporary tableware

Dish Factory Outlet
dishfactory.com
213-687-9500
restaurant ware

Fishs Eddy
fishseddy.com
212-420-9020
vintage restaurant ware

Gorham
gorham1831.com
800-446-7426
Classic tableware

JC Penney
jcpenney.com
800-322-1189

Lenox
lenox.com
800-223-4311
china, accessories

Libbey
libbey.com
888-794-8469
glassware

Macy's
macys.com
800-289-6229

Match
match1995.com
201-792-9444
pewter, porcelain

Michael Aram
michaelaram.com
866-792-ARAM
botanical patterns

Michael C. Fina
michaelcfina.com
1-800-BUY-FINA
fine tableware, registry

Mikasa
mikasaandcompany.com
866-645-2721
contemporary collections

Reed and Barton
reedandbarton.com
800-343-1383
flatware, tableware

Replacements
replacements.com
800-737-5223
hard-to-find tableware

Saro Trading Company
saro.com
800-662-7276
crocheted doilies

Sur la Table
surlatable.com
800-243-0852
china, kitchenware

Waterford
waterford.com
800-955-1550
crystal, tableware

Wedgwood
wedgwoodusa.com
fine china, tableware

credits

TITLE PAGE: Compote, Crate & Barrel. Glassware, Libbey. Candles, Target. Coasters, Zelda Tannenbaum, Hollis Hills Mill.

PARTY BASICS

PAGE 14: Stemless flutes, Libbey. Crystal appliqués, Swarovski.

PAGE 16: Paper stock, Paper Access. Wax stamps, ink, pens, and nibs, Pearl Paint.

PAGE 17: Embosser, Scribes Delight. Rubber Stamps, Michaels.

PAGE 20: Tools, Jamali Garden Supplies. Oasis, Save on Crafts.

PAGE 25: Assorted candles, Creative Candles and Jamali Garden Supplies. LED candles, The Electric Candle Company.

PAGE 26: Glass votives, Jamali Garden Supplies. Self-inking rubber stamp, Impress Rubber Stamps. Ribbons, Michaels. Googly eyes, Michaels. Stickers, Paper Access. Vinyl decals, Wonderfulgraffiti.com. Metal leaf, Pearl Paint. Block letter, Jo-Ann Fabric and Craft Stores. Wallpaper trim, Walnut Wallpaper. Grapevine, Pany's

PAGE 29: Shaker, flowerpot vase, Marc Jacobs for Waterford. Decanter, Kate Spade. Scoop, tongs, Crate & Barrel.

PAGE 31: Bar tools, Crate & Barrel.

PAGE 32: Martini glass, Mikasa.

PAGE 33: Flutes, Libbey. Sugars, Wilton.

PAGE 34: Glassware, Mikasa.

PAGE 37: Glassware, Waterford.

PAGE 39: Wine glasses, Robert Mondavi by Waterford.

PAGE 41: Goblets, Waterford. Bowl, Crate & Barrel. Accent and dinner plate, Jasper Conran for Wedgwood. Flatware, Reed & Barton. Napkin, Ann Gish

PAGE 42: Dinner plates, napkins, flutes, Crate & Barrel.

PAGE 45: Shakers, Chef's Restaurant Supply.

NEW YEAR'S EVE

PAGES 48–49: Ornaments, Masco Florist Supplies.

PAGE 50: Vase, Jamali Garden Supplies. Flat-back crystals, Swarovski Crystal Components. Metal star confetti, Design Ideas.

PAGE 53: Frame, Target. Flutes, Libbey.

PAGE 54: Urn, Jamali Garden Supplies. Glassware, Libbey. Candelabra, Match.

PAGE 57: Flatware, Michael Aram.

PAGE 59: Shot glasses, Crate & Barrel. Pedestal cake plate, Abigails.

PAGE 60: Glass, Waterford. Spoon, Michael Aram. Coaster, Zelda Tannenbaum, Hollis Hills Mill.

PAGE 63: Votives, Jamali Garden Supplies. Tray, Tyler Florence by Mikasa.

LUNAR NEW YEAR

PAGE 64: Faux coral, Z Gallerie. Votives, Jamali Garden Supplies.

PAGE 67: Lanterns, Pearl River. Ribbons, Midori. Gold leaf, Pearl Paint.

PAGE 68: Coin, chopsticks, Pearl River. Ribbon, Midori.

PAGE 71: Origami paper, bamboo skewers, Pearl River.

PAGE 72: Martini glass, Mikasa. Gold leaf flakes, Easy Leaf. Joss paper, Pearl River.

PAGE 75: Snacks and Joss paper, Pearl River. Containers, The Container Store.

PAGE 76: Plate, Lenox. Bamboo steamer, chopsticks, Joss paper, Pearl River.

PAGE 79: Sake bottles, cups, Pearl River.

PAGE 80: Joss paper, bamboo candles, Pearl River. Mixing glasses, Target. Adhesive-back felt, Michaels.

VALENTINE'S DAY

PAGE 82: Conversation hearts, Candywarehouse.com.

PAGE 88: Flutes, Libbey. Tray, Tyler Florence for Mikasa.

PAGE 90: Bowl, Crate & Barrel. Flatware, Reed & Barton. Plate, Murval. Napkin, throw, Ann Gish.

PAGES 92–93: Coffee cups, Eternity by Wedgwood. Coffee Press, Bodum.

SPRING FLING

PAGES 96–97: Compote, Crate & Barrel.

PAGE 98: Glassware, Libbey. Rubber Stamp, Impressions Rubber Stamp.

PAGE 102: Plate, Lenox. Flatware, Reed & Barton.

PAGE 105: Wood paddles, Michaels.

PAGE 106: Plate, Lenox. Mini cupcakes, Whole Foods.

EARTH DAY

PAGE 108: Place mat, Zelda Tannenbaum, Hollis Hills Mill.

PAGE 111: Teak flatware, Viva Terra.

PAGE 114: Peat pot, Jiffy Pots.

PAGE 118: Votive glasses, Libbey. Tray, Bambu.

CINCO DE MAYO

PAGE 128: Plate, Bambu. Glass, Green Glass.

PAGE 130: Guatemalan tablecloth, Mango Trading. Glass bowl, 28th Street Marketplace.

PAGE 133: Plates, Lenox Butler's Pantry. Kitchen towels as napkins, Crate & Barrel. Guatemalan runner, Mango Trading.

PAGE 134: Acrylic martini glasses, Precidio.

PAGE 138: Twine bottle bags, Joneses Glasses, Libbey.

FLAG DAY

PAGE 142: Pitcher, Libbey.

PAGE 145: Frame used as tray, Target.

PAGE 146: Parasol, Big Sky Tents.

PAGE 149: Glass, Waterford.

PAGE 150: Plate, kitchen towel, Crate & Barrel. Fisherman's bracelet, Nantucket Knotworks.

PAGE 153: Plate, Fishs Eddy. Scallop shell, Williams Sonoma. Beach glass, Jamali Garden Supplies.

PAGE 154: Water, Saratoga.

PAGE 157: Bowl, Libbey. Candles, candlesjustonline.com. Beach glass, Jamali Garden Supplies.

LABOR DAY

PAGE 158: Green glass vase, Fire & LIght.

PAGE 162: Glassware, Arté Italica. Frame as tray, Target.

PAGE 163: Brander, Brand-first.

PAGE 165: Soda, Boylan Bottleworks.

PAGE 166: Clear bottles, Homebrew Adventures. Monogram decal, Wonderful Graffiti.com.

PAGE 168: Glass, Arté Italica. Plate, Fishs Eddy.

PAGE 172: Cast-iron pot, Lodge.

PAGE 175: Glassware, Arté Italica. Tray, Bambu.

HALLOWEEN

PAGE 178: Framed canvas, Pearl Paint. Hurricane, Accents de Ville.

PAGE 181: Coral fan, Dry Nature.

PAGE 182: Doily, Saro at L'artisana.com. Vase, Ikea.

PAGE 185: Gold Leaf, goldleaf.net.

PAGE 186: Glass mugs, Libbey. Tray, Bambu.

PAGE 189: Carafe, Kate Spade. Glass vase, Marc Jacobs for Waterford. Measuring bowl, Anchor Hocking.

PAGE 190: Bowl, Libbey.

THANKSGIVING

PAGE 194: Stone vase, Jamali. Faux grapes, Allstate Floral & Craft

PAGE 198: Glassware, Robert Mondavi for Waterford.

PAGE 201: Cheeses, Whole Foods

PAGE 202: Glassware, Mikasa.

PAGE 205: Plate, Butler's Pantry by Lenox. Cotton doily, Saro at L'artisana.com. Napkin, Crate & Barrell.

PAGE 206: Mini Mason jars, The Container Store. Tray, Bambu. Paper napkin, Seventh Generation.

PAGE 209: Votive, Libbey

WINTER SOLSTICE

PAGE 212: Grapevine balls, Dry Nature.

PAGE 215: Ribbons, Midori. Wreath ring, Afloral.com.

PAGE 216: Stone urn, Jamali Garden Supplies. Starfish, Dry Nature.

PAGE 219: Mini birdhouse, Michaels.

PAGE 220: Flute, Robert Mondavi byWaterford. Ornament, Michaels.

PAGE 223: Wineglass, Mikasa.

PAGE 224: China, Wedgwood. Sterling flatware, Vera Wang for Wedgewood.

PAGE 227: Mug, Crate & Barrel. Ribbon, Midori.

PARTY REGISTRY

PAGE 228: China, Marc Jacobs for Waterford. Place mat, napkin, Crate & Barrel.

RESOURCES

PAGE 231: Ribbon, Midori. Scissors, Pearl River.

acknowledgments

I can't tell you how good it feels to write these final words. This book has been a year in the making and I relied on so many talented, wonderful people to put this book together.

Thank you, Alison Rosa; your feisty spirit and keen eye made the creation of this beautiful book a joy. I thank the dynamic duo, Roy Galaday and Kevin Thomasson, our photo assistants, who kept two demanding women satisfied and laughing, not an easy feat. Susi Oberhelman has done it again. This is our fourth book together—thank you for designing another elegant, fresh home for my ideas. Your eagle eye caught many a gremlin even late, late at night. Janis Donnaud and Kathryn Huck, thanks for encouraging me to step beyond bridal and believing in this book. Thanks to Donna Cohen for polishing my prose and punctuation with precision. I am especially grateful for my wonderful assistants Machell Espejo and Christina Gould and for the invaluable studio management by Lori Kramerson and set assistants Hillary Launey, Ryan Karels, Lauren Sheehan, Amanda DeCamp, and Claudia Pedala, all of whom helped me keep sane. And to my own Brett, Ryan, and Evan, as ever, thanks.